BACH'S MAJOR VOCAL WORKS

BACH'S MAJOR VOCAL WORKS

MUSIC, DRAMA, LITURGY

MARKUS RATHEY

YALE UNIVERSITY PRESS
NEW HAVEN AND LONDON

For information about this and other Yale University Press publications, please contact:
U.S. office: sales.press@yale.edu   www.yalebooks.com
Europe Office: sales@yaleup.co.uk   www.yalebooks.co.uk

Typeset in Adobe Caslon Pro by IDSUK (DataConnection) Ltd
Printed in Great Britain by Gomer Press Ltd, Llandysul, Ceredigion, Wales

Library of Congress Cataloging-in-Publication Data

Rathey, Markus, author.
    Johann Sebastian Bach : the major vocal works / Markus Rathey.
        pages cm
    Includes bibliographical references and index.
    ISBN 978-0-300-21720-9 (alk. paper)
1. Bach, Johann Sebastian, 1685-1750. Vocal music. I. Title.
ML410.B13R29 2016
    782.2'2092—dc23

                                                                    2015035258

A catalogue record for this book is available from the British Library.

10 9 8 7 6 5 4 3 2 1

I submit in deepest devotion the present small work
of that science which I have achieved in *musique*.
J. S. Bach, 1733

Nil canitur suavius, nil auditur jucundius.
Hymn 'Jesu dulcis memoria'

CONTENTS

ACKNOWLEDGEMENTS

This book has grown over more than a decade. During the past twelve years at the Yale Institute of Sacred Music I had the opportunity to teach courses on Johann Sebastian Bach's vocal music, to coach conductors and singers how to perform these pieces, and to give public lectures on Bach's oratorios, passions and his *B Minor Mass*. Collaborating with conductors such as Masaaki Suzuki, Helmuth Rilling, David Hill, Marguerite Brooks, and Simon Carrington has given me invaluable insights into the music.

Most of the chapters in this book have started as pre-concert lectures for performances at Yale and other places, such as the Bach Festival at Baldwin Wallace University (Berea, OH). Writing program notes for numerous ensembles and performances has encouraged me to write texts that are also accessible to non-musicians. Three ensembles I have collaborated with for several years now and which have inspired me with their performances are the Yale Schola Cantorum (since 2003), the Yale Camerata (since 2004), and the Chicago Bach Project (since 2011). I should also mention the Bach Collegium Japan. Not only has Masaaki Suzuki been a wonderful colleague for several years but his recordings of Bach's music have also accompanied my work on most of the chapters.

I am grateful to colleagues and friends who have read parts or all of the manuscript and who have given me valuable comments and suggestions: Kathryn Aaron, Danielle Annett, Stephen Crist, Mark Peters, James Taylor, and Thomas Troeger. My research assistant, Emilie Coakley, has edited the manuscript meticulously. I am also grateful to the anonymous readers for Yale University Press, whose constructive remarks have helped make the argument in this book even stronger. Robert Baldock, Rachael Lonsdale, and Candida Brazil at Yale University Press have supported me in this project and have overseen a smooth and efficient production process.

I am indebted to my students and colleagues at the Yale Institute of Sacred Music for their scholarship and support, the inspiration of their music-making, their passion for the visual and literary arts, and the countless conversations, both in class and outside the classroom. This book is dedicated to them.

Markus Rathey
New Haven, October 2015

A NOTE ON TRANSLATIONS

The translations of the texts for Bach's oratorios are based on Michael Marissen, *Bach's Oratorios. The Parallel German-English Texts with Annotations* (Oxford: Oxford University Press, 2008). Translations of texts from Bach's cantatas follow Alfred Dürr, *The Cantatas of J. S. Bach*, trans. Richard D. P. Jones (Oxford: Oxford University Press, 2005). All other translations (especially of theological texts from the seventeenth and eighteenth centuries) are mine unless stated otherwise.

CHAPTER ONE

PRELUDE

Towards the beginning of the second decade of the nineteenth century, the London-based *New Monthly Magazine and Literary Journal* published a rather odd description of Johann Sebastian Bach's oratorios:

> Bach, too, is said to have written Oratorios of the highest merit; but, in this particular, we are under the necessity of taking the word of his biographer [Johann Nikolaus Forkel]. We are not acquainted with them; indeed they are little known, and probably were planned on a limited scale. But we can fully imagine what he might have produced in this department, by referring to some sacred compositions that have come under our notice. A solemn, pious simplicity, is their distinguishing feature; they abound with melodies of the most select and elevated cast; the accompaniments are of the first order; and the choruses, although on a more limited scale than Handel's, are equally grand and impressive.[1]

We smile about this anonymous author's attempt to imagine what Johann Sebastian Bach's oratorios might have sounded or looked like. The article comes with a preconceived notion of the composer that is based on his works for keyboard and the few vocal works (especially the motets) that had come to light. It is 1821 and we are still eight years away from Felix Mendelssohn Bartholdy's performance of the *St Matthew Passion* in 1829, which will mark the return of Bach's music to the public sphere. Bach and his music had never been entirely forgotten. However, his only music that was widely known and available at the time was his keyboard works, which were studied by composers and pianists alike. We cannot blame this British author for trying to accomplish an impossible task: to extrapolate the character of Bach's oratorios based on works such as the *Well-tempered Clavier* or his motets. A few of his assumptions are even spot-on, like the "most select and elevated" melodies and the "grand and impressive" choruses. At other times the author is misled by preconceived notions. Works like the *St Matthew Passion* or the *Christmas Oratorio* were clearly not planned on a "limited scale." Neither are most of Bach's choruses on a "more limited scale than Handel's."

But the mention of Handel in this context points to one of the problems this author had to deal with. The English notion of baroque music was dominated by the works of George Frideric Handel (1685–1759). His oratorios were a national musical treasure and works by other composers like Bach had to be described and understood in relation to the standards set by Handel. Very soon, music historiography established a view of Bach and Handel as polar opposites—Handel as the international and extroverted composer and Bach as the German and introverted cantor and keyboardist. Another quotation from our article reflects this view:

Bach's character was cast in a widely different mould: his modesty, his almost infantine simplicity, was free from any pretensions; to vanity and ambition he was an utter stranger. He moved, with perfect contentment, in the narrowed orbit of a few petty German courts, contiguous to each other—for he loved his art more than fame. Thus circumstanced, we are not to wonder that he wrote little for a full orchestra, but devoted his genius and his time, almost exclusively, to the organ and clavichord.[2]

Obvious misconceptions like Bach's "almost infantine simplicity" or the lack of works for full orchestra are again due to the author's limited knowledge (based on the works accessible in 1821) of Bach's music. However, the view of Bach's character and music that is expressed here explains why the author was led to assume that Bach's oratorios had to be on a much smaller scale than Handel's.[3]

Today's listeners know more about Bach and his vocal works, but we still come with certain preconceived notions and expectations. They might be more informed than the article from 1821, but we nevertheless have an image of Bach that we want to see confirmed in the oratorios, passions, and cantatas we hear in concerts and other performances. The anonymous author's article poses the intriguing question: what characterizes Bach's major vocal works? Why did Bach compose them? What was the original function of his oratorios, passions, the masses, and the *Magnificat*? The title of this book locates the works within the context of "Drama" and "Liturgy." Bach's major works were composed for use in Lutheran worship services; they are liturgical pieces with a specific function within the order of the service. Even the *B Minor Mass*, which was never performed by Bach in a service, follows the structure of the liturgy. While being designed for the liturgy, the vocal works are also highly dramatic, but not in the sense that an opera is dramatic. The works were not staged, and we rarely have the dialogues between protagonists that would qualify as dramatic action. However, Bach's compositions highlight the dramatic and emotional potential of the texts: joy and sadness, fear and hope, longing and desire. Like in eighteenth-century opera, love is one of the major topics of Bach's vocal works. We find love songs and amorous duets in his *Magnificat*, his passions, the *Christmas Oratorio*, and the *B Minor Mass*, which features no fewer than three love duets. Bach never composed an opera but he did know how to set an effective love scene to music! The idea of Bach as composer of love duets would have been utterly foreign to our anonymous author from 1821. It would have been Handelian but not Bachian.

The six introductions to Bach's major vocal works in this book are geared toward music lovers who want to read about a piece before going to a performance or before listening to a recording. The chapters can be read independently or in the sequence in which they appear. Readers will discover how certain musical and theological ideas recur in several large-scale works by Bach. Each chapter tries to give the reader some pointers on what to listen for in the music. In a short book like this it is impossible to provide a complete description of each movement. Instead, I am focusing on a few central aspects in each piece that help one to hear the movements within a larger framework. The chapters do not follow the chronological order in which Bach composed the works (for a chronology see Appendix A at the end of the book). Rather, this book is arranged to show the compositions according to the chronology of the life of Christ—which is also the order of the liturgical year: the announcement of Christ's coming in the

Magnificat, the birth of Christ in the *Christmas Oratorio*, his suffering and death in the passions according to John and Matthew, his resurrection in the *Easter Oratorio*, and his return to the father in the *Ascension Oratorio*. The *B Minor Mass* forms the final bookend. The text of the mass is a summary of the Christian faith—and, coincidentally, the mass is also a culmination of Bach's own work.

The first introduction presents Bach's settings of the Song of Mary, the *Magnificat*. It shows how Bach highlights the female voice and how he employs gender typologies to convey the message of the biblical canticle. I have included in that chapter a description of the chorale cantata *Meine Seel' erhebt den Herren* BWV 10, which is based on the German text of the *Magnificat*. This piece in the vernacular can help highlight some of the peculiarities of Bach's understanding of the *Magnificat*. Such a comparison also allows us to explore the two primary venues for Bach's vocal works: the morning service on Sundays and feast days (for which BWV 10 was composed); and the vespers service, the original place for the large, Latin *Magnificat*. We will return to these two venues throughout the rest of the book.

The chapter on Bach's *Christmas Oratorio* explores the relationship between Bach's interest in operatic scenes, as we can see them in his secular cantatas, and his setting of the nativity story. He borrowed some of the movements from secular works and integrated them into his oratorio. Love songs turn into lullabies and allusions to the consummation of carnal desire are transformed into a praise of divine mercy. Seen from this perspective, Bach's *Christmas Oratorio* appears as a gigantic love story that traces the arrival of the "beloved bridegroom," Christ, in the believer's heart.

The two passions, composed by Bach during his early years in Leipzig, each have a different character. The account of the suffering in the Gospel according to John is shaped by a view of the death of Christ as a demonstration of his divine glory. Accordingly, the setting by Bach is bookended by movements that celebrate God as the ruler of the world. The Gospel according to Matthew, on the other hand, is more interested in the human side of Jesus' suffering, and so is the setting of this story by Bach. Bach's *St Matthew Passion* interprets the death of Christ as a manifestation of divine love. As in the *Christmas Oratorio*, the image of the divine bridegroom abounds. Listeners can already encounter this view in the majestic opening movement of the passion, in which the Daughter of Zion admonishes the Faithful to behold the bridegroom.

The two smaller oratorios for Easter Sunday and Ascension Day are often neglected, in part due to their size. They were composed for use during the regular morning liturgy and consequently are much shorter than their sister compositions. Here, my overview focuses on a common theme in both oratorios, the relationship between seeing and understanding. It was a theme that was of great interest to Enlightenment philosophers and theologians during the early eighteenth century and the relationship between empiricism, rationalism, and Christian tradition were widely discussed in Bach's time. While the oratorios are not designed as a contribution to this philosophical discourse, they do represent a particular position within the ongoing discussion.

When Bach dispatched to the court in Dresden the *Kyrie* and *Gloria* of what would later become the *B Minor Mass*, he accompanied the first two parts of the mass with a letter that identified the pieces as a "small work of that science which [he had] achieved in *musique*." In other words, this was a representative sample of his accomplishments as a composer. When Bach completed the mass in the late 1740s it still retained the character of a summary and culmination of his vocal works. My overview of the mass in Chapter Seven elaborates on the exemplary character of the mass and again highlights two elements: the use of operatic drama as a tool for the interpretation of the text and the large-scale architecture of the mass, which shows Bach's interest in balance and proportion.

The chapters of this book are written with a general audience in mind. Musical training is not required and I have tried to avoid musicological jargon. The most important technical terms are explained in a short glossary at the end of the book. The musical examples have been selected so that even readers without profound musical knowledge can visually decipher most of the examples: ascending lines are immediately visible, as are those moments in the music when suddenly all accompanying instruments drop out and the score looks "empty." I encourage the reader to have a look at the music examples as graphic elements, even if they cannot translate the notes into sound. There is still a lot to see and discover in a Bach score!

The chapters of this book are conceived as introductions, guides for informed listening. The music examples the book contains cannot and will not replace listening to the entire piece. It is my hope that reading about the works will encourage readers to attend a performance of a passion, to sit down with a recording of the *Ascension Oratorio*, or to sing the *B Minor Mass* with a choir.

CHAPTER TWO

A FEMALE VOICE

MARY IN BACH'S *MAGNIFICAT* SETTINGS BWV 243 AND 10

You regard me in my lowliness (BWV 10/2)

Most of the citizens of Leipzig knew Johann Sebastian Bach as a composer of music for the liturgy. Even after taking over the *Collegium Musicum* in 1729—an ensemble of instrumentalists of mostly university students, which performed regularly in a local coffee house—the more than 120 church services for which Bach was responsible each year dwarfed all other performances. Bach had been employed in Leipzig since 1723 as church musician and teacher. That meant he served as cantor at the two main churches, taught the boys at the school that was affiliated with the St Thomas church, and was also responsible for sacred music at several other churches of the city.[1] In the two major churches, St Thomas and St Nicholas, he had to perform cantatas, passions, and other vocal works on a regular basis.

Things have changed since the 1720s. While we still regard Bach as a composer of sacred music, his major pieces have moved from the church to the concert hall, or at least from the liturgy to extra-liturgical performances in churches that serve as concert spaces. However, when listening to Bach's music, it is important to keep in mind that his most celebrated works, his passions, the *Christmas Oratorio*, the *Magnificat*, and the smaller oratorios for Easter and Ascension, were composed for use in worship services. They fulfill a specific function in these services and interact with other liturgical elements, much like readings, hymns, or the sermon. This chapter will explore two settings of the *Magnificat*, the praise of Mary, a festive, Latin *Magnificat*, composed during Bach's first year in Leipzig, and a German chorale cantata based on the same text. The two pieces are not only musically distinct, but they also represent two distinct forms of worship services, mass and vespers. As all of Bach's large-scale works were written for one of these services, the exploration of their liturgical contexts will also set the stage for the remaining works in this book.

Beginnings

Johann Sebastian Bach's first major piece, after beginning his tenure in Leipzig in 1723, was not a passion or an oratorio, but rather a setting of the Latin text of the Song of Mary, the *Magnificat*, from the first chapter of the Gospel according to Luke. The text is part of the narrative that leads up to the nativity: Mary, already pregnant with Jesus, visits her elderly relative Elizabeth, who at this time is pregnant with John the Baptist. Elizabeth feels the special significance of Mary's child and praises her. In response, Mary speaks (or sings) the following text:

> *My soul magnifies the Lord,*
> *and my spirit rejoices in God my Savior,*
> *for he has looked with favor on the lowliness of his servant.*
> *See, from now on all generations will call me blessed;*
> *for the Mighty One has done great things for me,*
> *and holy is his name.*

His mercy is for those who fear him
from generation to generation.
He has shown strength with his arm;
he has scattered the proud in the thoughts of their hearts.
He has brought down the powerful from their thrones,
and lifted up the lowly;
he has filled the hungry with good things,
and sent the rich away empty.
He has helped his servant Israel,
in remembrance of his mercy,
according to the promise he made to our ancestors,
to Abraham and to his descendants for ever.

The choice of this piece was not Bach's alone. It rather was a necessity within the liturgical year. Bach's tenure had started on May 30, 1723,[2] and the first major feast day was the Visitation of Mary on July 2, 1723, for which a festive rendition of the *Magnificat* was needed. However, Bach was not necessarily obligated to perform a composition from his own pen. He could have used a piece from the rich repertoire of *Magnificat* compositions—as he would sometimes do in later years.[3] But instead he chose to present himself to his new audience with a new composition of his own.[4] As far as we know, the entire piece was newly composed and did not use older material Bach had written in Weimar or Köthen.

The *Magnificat* was the musical highlight of the vespers service. The vespers as the evening service of the Christian church had a long tradition, dating back to the early Middle Ages. The service had originally included (and in the Catholic tradition still does) a sequence of several psalms and prayers, and culminated in the singing of the *Magnificat*. As with the psalms during the vespers service, the singing of the Song of

Mary ended with the lesser doxology, the invocation of the trinity ("Gloria patri, et filii …"). This tradition was maintained in Bach's Latin and German *Magnificats* as well.

During the Reformations of the sixteenth century, churches such as the Lutheran Church and the Anglican Church borrowed this structure of daily services and revised it for their own purposes. In the Church of England, the vespers became the model for Evensong, while the vespers service in the Lutheran tradition became a service in the early afternoon, which centered on a sermon. However, both the churches in England and in the Lutheran territories maintained the *Magnificat* as an essential part of the liturgy. In Bach's Leipzig, the vespers service would have had the following structure:[5]

Organ Prelude
Hymn
Cantata (repeated from morning service, on feast days only)
Hymn of the day
Psalm
Lord's prayer
Hymn
Announcement of the sermon
Hymn: *Herr Jesu Christ, dich zu uns wend'*
Scripture reading
Sermon
Prayers
Magnificat
Responsory, collect, and benediction
Hymn: *Nun danket alle Gott*

The vespers were celebrated in Leipzig on Saturday evening, on Sunday afternoons and before high feast days. One special vespers service during the year was the vespers on Good Friday afternoon, during which Bach performed his passions.[6] We will return to this service in a later chapter. On a feast day, Bach would usually have repeated the main cantata from the morning service and then, in the second half of the vespers, the congregation would have heard a setting of the Song of Mary. Festive *Magnificats* were an exception. On a normal Sunday, the text was sung in a simple four-part setting and in German. Only on feast days did the choir perform a Latin version with elaborate instrumental accompaniment.

Johann Sebastian Bach's *Magnificat* has a complex history. The earliest version that is extant is a version in E flat major (BWV 243a), which also features interpolated songs for Christmas. Interpolations like this had been quite usual. We find examples already in the early seventeenth century in works by composers like Michael Praetorius (1571–1621). This version was performed during Bach's first Christmas feast in Leipzig on December 25, 1723.[7] However, Bach scholar Andreas Glöckner has recently shown that this version already existed earlier and that it was performed without Christmas interpolations on the Feast of the Visitation 1723.[8] Thus, Bach would have composed the piece shortly after he had moved to Leipzig. He then interpolated the Christmas songs when he performed the composition again about half a year later.[9]

Bach might have performed that E flat major *Magnificat* (with and without the interpolations) in the following years. Between 1728 and 1731 he revised the piece, adding flutes, correcting some compositional mistakes, smoothing the voice leading and the harmonic progression, and transposing the composition from E flat major down a half step to D major. The reason was probably because trumpets in D were more easily available than the rarer E flat trumpets. The Christmas interpolations are missing in this revised version and we can assume that this later piece was not specifically intended for a Christmas service.

And yet, even if performed on a different day, the *Magnificat* always retains a certain connection to Christmas, as the text was first sung by Jesus' mother, shortly before his birth. In Lutheran understanding, the Song of Mary (as Marian theology in general) is perceived from the perspective of Christological theology, and the *Magnificat* is thus a celebration of the incarnation.[10]

Tonus Peregrinus

As I mentioned earlier, on normal weekends, if no special feast day was celebrated, the *Magnificat* was sung in a simple four-part setting. The melody employed in Leipzig was a so-called psalm tone, a melodic model that was used to chant psalms or psalm-like texts such as the *Magnificat*. In the Lutheran tradition it had been a custom to chant the Song of Mary with the *tonus peregrinus*, a melodic model that has a characteristic twist: typically, each psalm tone consist of two halves. A middle cadence separates two static notes that are used to sing most of the text. Whereas in all other psalm tones, this long note has the same pitch in both halves, in the *tonus peregrinus*, the note in the second half is one step lower.[11] This renders this psalm tone immediately recognizable, and Bach uses it in several of his *Magnificat* compositions (example 2.1).

Magnificat in D Major BWV 243

The *Magnificat* is a piece about Christ's coming and the antic-ipation of his glorious arrival. Bach's work not only marks

Example 2.1: *Tonus Peregrinus*

Christ's arrival but also the composer's own arrival in Leipzig in 1723. He presents himself to his audience in the most splendid way: trumpets, a large ensemble, massive concerto movements, intimate arias, and a sweet, almost amorous duet. Some of these elements are even increased in the later, revised version—for instance, when he adds the sweet sound of the flutes to the sixth movement, "Et misericordia." Overall, Bach shows a great sense of the dramatic potential of the *Magnificat* text: praise, the dichotomy between glory and humility, the scattering of the proud, the elevation of the lowly, and the expression of God's mercy. Bach was not the first to do so. Since the early seventeenth century, composers such as Claudio Monteverdi, one of the fathers of opera, had appreciated how dramatic the Song of Mary had been and used this powerful language to their advantage.

In addition to the expressive setting of the text, Bach's *Magnificat* also betrays a great sense for musical architecture. Movements one and twelve serve as framing pillars for the entire piece. The two movements are connected on several levels. Their texts express a similar exuberant praise: "Magnificat anima mea" – "Gloria Patri" (My soul magnifies the Lord – Glory be to God the father). Bach returns verbatim to the musical themes from the opening movement for the final twenty-three measures of the last movement. This creates cyclical unity on a musical level, while also highlighting the textual similarities. We will see repeatedly that Bach is interested in a balance between text interpretation on the one hand and musical architecture on the other. The *B Minor Mass* is a fascinating exercise in this respect.

In the inner movements of the *Magnificat*, Bach alternates between celebratory tutti movements, engaging the entire ensemble, and more intimate arias for soloists. Quite regularly, a concerto movement is followed by two arias. Bach abandons this pattern only for the final three movements (nos. 10–12), creating a musical climax that finds its release in the return to the musical material from the opening.

The individual movements deserve a more detailed discussion. Bach opens the *Magnificat* with celebratory fanfares: the trumpets play broken triads while the other instruments create a complex web of 16th-note runs and broken chords. Within a few measures, the first trumpet establishes itself as a solo instrument and plays vivid 16th-note figurations. After thirty measures, about a third of the way into the opening movement, Bach introduces the vocalists with the text "Magnificat anima mea Dominum" (My soul magnifies the Lord). It is one of the rare cases in his oeuvre in which Bach uses a five-part chorus. The composer clearly wanted to present a splendid and magnificent piece.

Large sections of the vocal part are built into this mostly literal repetition of the instrumental opening. Bach scholars call this "Vokaleinbau" (vocal integration), a technique Bach uses quite frequently. What is more important for us here, however, is the dominance of the instruments. Not only does the movement begin with thirty measures of festive fanfares but it also ends with the instruments playing fifteen measures

of similar material. That means that about half of the movement is executed by the instruments alone. Bach celebrates the
praise of God through the sound of the instruments, through
music. The text makes this praise explicit, but the composer
clearly emphasizes the musical aspects of this praise. And
he uses instruments that most clearly express the powerful
domination of the "Lord:" the trumpets and the timpani.
These were considered royal instruments in Bach's time and
contemporary listeners would have been aware of these regal
connotations.

The music of the opening is a representation of a magnificent ruler. The following movement, an aria for the second
soprano and strings, is both a continuation of this effect and at
the same time a sharp contrast. The text clearly asked for
continuity: "and my spirit rejoices in God my Savior." But
musically, Bach needed diversity. So he gave the text to a soloist,
but the instruments (as well as the singer) keep using the
broken triads, the fanfares, from the beginning; still alternating
with vivid 16th-note motives. The movement feels like a vari-
ation of the opening, but on a smaller scale. We have seen in
the opening that the trumpets have a "meaning:" they signify
the king, the royal ruler-ship of God. The choice of the soprano
in the second movement has significance as well. The
Magnificat is the Song of Mary, the praise by a woman. By
using the soprano, Bach chose a voice register that typically
had female connotations—even though the part was originally
sung by a boy soprano. Of course, Bach is not intending to
represent Mary here. But the choice of the vocal register alludes
to the fact that we are listening to the song of a woman.[12]

The "other side" of this woman is highlighted in the next
movement, "Et exsultavit spiritus meus" (And my spirit
rejoices) (no. 3). Mary praises God but she herself is God's

humble maid. Bach now gives this text to the first soprano. In other words, the gender connotations of the voice register are still the same. While giving the part to another soloist (and thus giving the singer of the first aria some rest), Bach was not interested in a vocal contrast. Instead, contrast is established by other parameters such as key (B minor), tempo (Adagio), and the instrumental sound of the oboe d'amore. Bach paints the two faces of Mary: Mary the Mother of Christ who praises God for his deeds and Mary the humble maid who does what God has commanded. For Martin Luther and for Lutheran theologians after him, Mary is both a model in her praise of God, as well as in her humility.[13] Bach's setting is indeed humble. He refrains from longer melismas and assigns the singer a simpler, smooth, flowing melodic line. The prevalence of descending melodic phrases highlights this attitude of humility. This slightly changes in the second half of the aria, when the text gets increasingly excited: "Ecce" ("see!") is repeated four times in a row, and Bach combines it with ascending gestures that demand attention.

Mary's song of humility transitions seamlessly into the second choral movement (no. 4). The transition comes as a dramatic surprise. The surprise, as well as the change of texture, is warranted by the text: "omnes generationes" (from generation to generation, or more literally, "all generations".) It had been common since the seventeenth century to depict the word for "all" by bringing back the entire ensemble. We now hear all the generations singing together the praise of God. Bach adds to this impression through points of imitation in which one voice is following after the other. The listener can hear how the praise of God is handed from one generation to the next; one generation following the other. The visual impression is especially telling for this example (example 2.2).

Example 2.2: Bach, *Magnificat* BWV 243/4, mm. 9–12

The next pair of solo movements again sets up a contrast. Bach now juxtaposes a solo aria for bass (no. 5) and a duet for alto and tenor (no. 6). If Bach employed gender stereotypes in the two earlier solos to paint the two sides of Mary as the one who glorified God and as God's humble maid, he now manipulates gender stereotypes in a different way. The aria no. 5, "Quia fecit mihi magna," celebrates the "Mighty One." While the text is still spoken by Mary, the focus is not on her but on God and on his might. Power, might, and strength in the eighteenth century were not only divine but also masculine attributes.[14] Thus, Bach gives the text to the paradigmatic male voice, the bass, which is here only accompanied by the dark sound of the basso continuo. But it is not darkness Bach is going for. It is strength, virility, power. In extensive melismas, often spanning a wide range, the bass demonstrates his domination. It is the starkest contrast to Mary's humility in movement no. 3.

The sixth movement, "Et misericordia," explores gender dynamics in yet another way. The text obviously deals with God's mercy. But we have to understand that in eighteenth-century Protestant theology, divine mercy was viewed as an expression of divine love. God acted mercifully because he loved the world. The following sequence of movements from the third part of Bach's *Christmas Oratorio*, composed about a decade after the *Magnificat*, makes this connection very clear:

Movement 27

Er hat sein Volk *getröst'* ...	He has comforted his people ...
Die Hülf aus *Zion* hersendet	Sent salvation out from Zion
Und *unser Leid geendet.*	And ended our suffering

Movement 28

Dies hat er alles uns getan,	All this he has done for us,
Sein groß Lieb zu zeigen an …	To show his great love …

Movement 29

Herr, dein *Mitleid*, dein Erbarmen …	Lord, your compassion, your mercy …
Tröstet uns und macht uns frei.	Comforts us and makes us free.
Deine holde Gunst und *Liebe* …	Your pleasing favor and love …

The last movement in the above example, the duet no. 29, manifests this connection by combining a text about divine compassion with music that had originally been composed as an erotic love duet in one of Bach's secular cantatas (see Chapter Three). Love and mercy, as Bach's setting expresses, are intrinsically intertwined.[15] Typical features of love duets in Bach's time (and in the duet from the *Christmas Oratorio*) are the use of male and female voice registers (even if all sung by men), parallel movement in harmonious sixths and thirds, and an overall "sweet" sound that could be created by melodic simplicity or the use of instruments like oboi d'amore (love oboes) or flutes. All this is the case for the sixth movement in the *Magnificat*. Bach combines the two gendered voices that are closest to each other, alto and tenor. While this combination is less frequent than the combination of soprano and bass in Bach's sacred love duets, it does create the sense of particular intimacy and sweetness. The voices move in close, harmonious thirds and sixths, as do the accompanying instruments. The entire movement is a celebration of harmony and affection. It is a sacred love duet that highlights God's mercy as an act and expression of his love.

We might even dare go one step further: the movement not only features the two singers in sweet harmony but the lilting 12/8 meter is characteristic of this duet sound, combined with a slowly pulsating instrumental bass voice. Listeners familiar with Bach's music might be reminded of the opening movement of his *St Matthew Passion*, which exhibits similar rhythmical characteristics (see Chapter Five). These associations are not far-fetched. The text for the opening movement for the passion features the Daughter of Zion who is waiting for Christ the bridegroom. We will see in the following chapters that the image of love is central to the theology of Christ's passion in Bach's time. The suffering and death of Christ were seen as an expression of God's mercy.

With movement six of the *Magnificat*, Bach has introduced his five soloists with individual movements: the two sopranos have highlighted the two sides of Mary, the bass has celebrated divine strength and power, and alto and tenor have indulged in the harmonious sounds of a sacred love duet. The following tutti movement, the third of the *Magnificat*, now puts them all back together in one movement. Each of the five voices has an extensive, melismatic solo that is pitted against the backdrop of a more homophonic texture in the remaining voices. The opening measures already make this very clear (example 2.3). The topic is again power, here the power of the divine arm that scatters the proud. The most surprising moment comes towards the end of the chorus: "He has scattered the proud in the thoughts of their hearts." Bach indeed "scatters" his notes and lightens the hitherto very dense texture. At measure 28 Bach suddenly arrives in an unexpected key (a diminished chord on *E sharp*!), followed by a long rest in all voices. The proud were scattered and have dissolved into nothing. This rest signifies the "nothing," the annihilation of sound, and thus of all being.[16] The movement ends in a harmonically rich adagio setting of the words "proud in the thoughts of their hearts."

Example 2.3: Bach, *Magnificat* BWV 243/7, mm. 1–4

The last two solo movements are given to the two voices
that had not had individual soli, the alto and the tenor. This
shows that Bach, while using gendered stereotypes associated
with specific voices to his advantage, also thinks pragmatically
and gives every singer relatively the same amount of work to
do.[17] The tenor aria "Deposuit" (He has brought down the
powerful) stages the bringing down of the mighty from their
thrones with rapid descending lines, while the lowly are lifted
up with gradually ascending melismas. Like so many composers
before him, Bach uses the spacial juxtaposition provided by
the text to create music that traverses the space of the musical
score. Bach once more exhibits his keen sense for a dramatic
text interpretation.

The subject of the alto aria "Esurientes implevit" (He has
filled the hungry) is a dichotomy of a different kind. Now it is
not the difference between high and low, but rather the juxtaposition of fullness (of the hungry) and emptiness (of the rich).
The instrumental introduction (ritornello) begins with "full"
harmonies: parallel movements in the two flutes as we know
them from the "sweet" love duets. Everything is harmonious,
the world is restored to order and harmony. However, the
voices get scattered when the text mentions the emptiness the
rich have to expect at the end of time. The sweet and full
texture dissolves into ragged motives and the accompaniment
drops out entirely in mm. 34/35 (example 2.4). And even the
short instrumental postlude ends with a single and forlorn
bass note. Musical emptiness!

The next movement (no. 10)—a somewhat strange motet-
like setting for two sopranos, alto, oboes, and basso continuo—
slowly reclaims this empty space: the instrumental bass begins as
the previous movement had ended, with a single note. But
immediately, the first soprano conquers the musical space

Example 2.4: Bach, *Magnificat* BWV 243/9, mm. 34–36

upwards, followed by alto, which expands the sound in a downward motion. The second soprano enters one measure later while the basso continuo grounds the texture with a pulsating bass line. The most surprising moment occurs in measure 5, when the two oboes suddenly play the melody of the *tonus peregrinus* on top of the polyphonic vocal texture. As I mentioned earlier, the familiar psalm tone was commonly used during vespers to chant the *Magnificat*. But Bach had so far not quoted the chorale melody in this festive setting. He now introduces this reminiscence as a climactic moment, shortly before the piece comes to an end. We will see in cantata BWV 10 that Bach does a similar thing in his German *Magnificat* one year later.

The "Sicut locutus est" (According to his promise) had commonly been set as a strict fugue and Bach does the same here. But the polyphonic texture comes to a halt on the word "Abraham," highlighting the name of the patriarch from the

Old Testament. The *Magnificat* ends with the lesser Doxology (*Gloria Patri*). After a homophonic declamation of the first word, the movement continues with a musical crescendo. Lines of ascending triplets claim the musical space from the low A up to F sharp, before Bach finally returns to the musical material from the opening movement. The juxtaposition of homophonic chords and perpetual triplet motion reminds one of the *Sanctus* from the *B Minor Mass*, which was composed shortly thereafter, for Christmas Day 1724.

Bach's *Magnificat* is an excellent example of the way the composer keeps a balance between text interpretation and musical independence, between drama and architecture. The setting of the text appears with an air of drama, pitting voices, gendered characters, against one another. At the same time, the use of voices also follows a logical pattern, which finally leads to the climactic glory of the final movements. The setting of the Song of Mary was an appropriate way for Bach to present himself and his music to a wider audience in 1723. It was the first large-scale piece Bach performed in Leipzig and it would remain (with some revisions) part of his repertoire for years to come.

Meine Seel' erhebt den Herren BWV 10

Bach returned in an intriguing way to the *Magnificat* during his Chorale Cantata Cycle. In 1724 Bach and an unknown librettist tackled an ambitious project, transforming congregational hymns into church cantatas. The project was abandoned prematurely, but Bach still wrote forty cantatas between June 11, 1724 and March 25, 1725. The basic pattern in each of the cantatas is the same: while the framing hymn stanzas were kept intact, the texts for the middle stanzas of each chorale were paraphrased, expanded, and sometimes combined with allusions to the readings for that particular Sunday or feast day.[18] For Bach, the chorale cantata was a compositional challenge. Especially in the opening movements he came up with a broad variety of compositional solutions, ranging from classical motets to concerti for orchestra and choir to settings that resemble an instrumental solo concerto (albeit with interpolated quotations from the hymn). Even in the middle movements—mostly arias and recitatives—Bach employed some very intriguing methods for combining the new text with quotations from the familiar hymn tunes.

The text for the chorale cantata *Meine Seel' erhebt den Herren* BWV 10 is based on the German translation of the biblical text of the *Magnificat*, but parts of the text now appear in paraphrase and with extensive interpretations. In contrast to the D Major *Magnificat*, which had been composed for the vespers service, the cantata was written for the morning service on the feast of the Visitation of Mary. Like the Latin *Magnificat* in the vespers, the cantata fulfilled a specific function within the liturgy of the mass service. Here is an outline of the structure of the services in Leipzig, sketched by Bach himself in 1723. Bach's outline is not complete but it lists the pieces that were most relevant for the musician:

Preluding [of the organ]
Motet
Preluding on the Kyrie, which is performed throughout in concerted manner
Intoning before the altar
Reading of the Epistle
Singing of the Litany

Preluding to [and signing of] the Chorale

Reading of the Gospel

Preluding on [and performance of] the principal music

[**Cantata**]

Singing of the Creed

The Sermon

After the Sermon, as usual, singing of several verses of a hymn

Words of Institution [of the Sacrament]

Preluding on [and performance of] the music [i.e. another concerted piece]. After the same, alternate preluding and singing of chorales until the end of the Communion, and so on.

The cantata was performed between the reading of the gospel text and the sermon (which was in turn based on the gospel). This positioning has an immediate impact on the cantata texts: very frequently the texts refer to the gospel or other readings from the liturgy and weave them together into something we might call a musical sermon. The cantatas are (to a large degree) musical meditations on the readings and the general themes of a Sunday, even before those themes are expounded in the sermon. In other words, the choice of a cantata and of a cantata text was not random, but rather it was closely embedded into the liturgy as a whole. Some of the large-scale compositions by Bach were composed for the same purpose and thus show a similar connection to the readings for the day (or at least to the main theme of the day): the *Christmas Oratorio*, the *Easter Oratorio*, and the *Ascension Oratorio*.

This can also be seen in cantata 10, *Meine Seel' erhebt den Herren*. The gospel reading for the day was Luke 1: 39–56, which contains in verses 46–54 the Song of Mary, the

Magnificat. The cantata was thus a direct reflection of the gospel lesson, building a bridge between the biblical reading and the sermon that was about to follow. Three of the seven movements of the cantata maintain the original biblical text, while the remaining movements, as common in Bach's chorale cantatas from 1724/5, paraphrase the text and expand it with interpretative interpolations. The words by the unknown librettist make the biblical text more concrete, insert images, and also infuse it with a Lutheran theology of redemption. The third movement, a recitative, makes this clear:

Biblical text	*Text for BWV 10/3*
Und seine Barmherzigkeit	Des Höchsten Güt und Treu
	Wird alle Morgen neu
währet immer für und für	Und währet immer für und für
bei denen,	Bei denen, die allhier
	Auf seine Hilfe schaun
die ihn fürchten.	Und ihm in wahrer Furcht
	vertraun.
Er übet Gewalt	Hingegen übt er auch Gewalt
mit seinem Arm	Mit seinem Arm
	An denen, welche weder kalt
	Noch warm
	Im Glauben und im Lieben sein;
	Die nacket, bloß und blind,
und zerstreuet die hoffärtig sind in ihres	Die voller Stolz und Hoffart sind,
Herzens Sinn.	Will seine Hand wie Spreu
	zerstreun.
His mercy is	The goodness and faithfulness of the Highest
	Are new every morning
	And last for ever and ever

for those who fear him	For those who here
from generation to generation.	Look up to his help
	And, in true fear, place their trust
	in him.
He has shown strength	On the other hand, he wields
	power
with his arm;	With his arm
	On those who are neither cold
	Nor warm
	In faith and in love;
	Naked, bare, and blind:
he has scattered the proud in the	Those who are full of pride and
thoughts of their hearts.	arrogance
	His hand will scatter like chaff.

It is not only God's mercy in general, but a very concrete mercy that is renewed every single morning, as the librettist adds with a reference to the biblical book of Lamentations (3:22–3). And the mercy is not only given to those who fear him, but who fear him *and* look to him for help. The next verse is even more expanded: what does the line "he has scattered the proud in the thoughts of their hearts" mean? What is "pride in our hearts?" Bach's librettist explains this in more tangible terms, again by including ideas from other biblical texts, in this case Revelation 3:16: "So, because you are luke-warm, and neither cold nor hot, I am about to spit you out of my mouth."

Movement six, another recitative, goes even further. The first half paraphrases the lines on God's promise to Abraham quite faithfully, but the second half inserts the incarnation of Christ, the fight against Satan, God's love as the foundation of his mercy, and finally the Lutheran keywords: Word of God, Mercy, and Truth:

Was Gott den Vätern alter Zeiten	What to the fathers in the days of old
Geredet und verheißen hat,	God spoke and pledged,
Erfüllt er auch im Werk und in der Tat.	He also fulfills in work and deed.
Was Gott dem Abraham,	What to Abraham,
Als er zu ihm in seine Hütten kam,	When he came to him in his tents,
Versprochen und geschworen,	God promised and swore
Ist, da die Zeit erfüllet war, geschehen.	Did happen when the fullness of time came:
Sein Same musste sich so sehr	His seed had to spread as much
Wie Sand am Meer	As sand at the sea
Und Stern am Firmament ausbreiten,	And stars in the firmament;
Der Heiland ward geboren,	The Savior was born,
Das ewge Wort ließ sich im Fleische sehen,	The eternal Word appeared in the flesh
Das menschliche Geschlecht von Tod und allem Bösen	To redeem the human race from death and all evil
Und von des Satans Sklaverei	And from Satan's slavery
Aus lauter Liebe zu erlösen;	Out of pure love;
Drum bleibt's darbei,	Therefore it remains the case
Dass Gottes Wort voll Gnad und Wahrheit sei.	That God's Word is full of grace and truth.

The text for the cantata is a little sermon on the *Magnificat* by itself. And Bach's music? The cantata begins with a vivid concerto-like movement. Not as celebratory as the Latin *Magnificat*, but still with a joyful character. When the voices enter after an instrumental introduction, the listener immediately recognizes the soprano melody: it is again the familiar beginning of the *tonus peregrinus*, the melodic model that was commonly used in Bach's church to chant the text of Mary's song of praise.

The following soprano aria is a celebration of bliss. The text is a praise of God and the joyful 16th-note motives and the ascending lines underscore this effect of joy. Listeners might even be reminded of some details from the Latin *Magnificat*, where we encountered similar ascending gestures. This is music that looks up in joyful expectation. And again it is the voice of the soprano, the female voice, which sings the first solo, just as in the Latin equivalent. We will see more similarities in the following movements. The music of the aria does not use the psalm tone—at least not directly. However, Bach alludes to one of its distinguishing features: one of the characteristics of a psalm tone is the cantilation tone, the single note that is repeated constantly and carries most of the text. If we look at the beginning of the soprano part, we see an unusually frequent repetition of single notes. These are not the exact notes we find in the psalm tone but Bach clearly plays with a stylistic feature of this familiar melody (example 2.5).

After a tenor recitative, Bach introduces the bass voice, which sings a paraphrase of the lines "He has brought down the powerful from their thrones" (no. 4). As in the Latin *Magnificat*, the demonstration of divine power and strength, here envisioned very concretely as physical strength, is given to the paradigmatic male voice, the bass. And it is again the bass with only the basso continuo. Wide-ranging melismas serve the celebration of male strength; connoisseurs of baroque opera will easily see the typical operatic rage aria: wide leaps, forceful melismas, dynamic force. The aria exudes testosterone. Like the previous aria, the bass does not quote the psalm tone, but again, we find an accumulation of note repetition in the opening material (example 2.6).

In his Latin *Magnificat* Bach had celebrated divine mercy as a manifestation of God's love. He had employed features of

Example 2.5: Bach, *Meine Seel' erhebt den Herren* BWV 10/2, mm. 13–16

Example 2.6: Bach, *Meine Seel' erhebt den Herren* BWV 10/4, mm. 1–3

the operatic love duet to stage this highly emotional moment in front of the eyes (and ears) of his listeners. In the cantata from 1724 this amorous moment appears a bit later in the piece, when the text talks about God's mercy for Israel. But the musical means are almost identical to the earlier composition:

alto and tenor, the male/female voice pair that is the closest, sing a movement in lilting triple meter, often moving in harmonious parallels. But Bach adds an interesting feature. In the Latin *Magnificat* he had set the text from this line with an unusual texture: three female voices sang the words, while an instrument played the *tonus peregrinus* on top of the polyphonic texture. Bach remembered what he had done a year earlier and now added the quotation of the psalm tone on top of his love duet. The result is an intriguingly beautiful piece. So intriguing, in fact, that more than a decade later Bach rewrote this very movement and turned it into an organ work.[19]

After the tenor recitative (no. 6) discussed earlier, the cantata ends with a simple, four-part chorale setting. The melody is again the *tonus peregrinus*, the familiar melody that was present in most of the movements from the cantata: it appeared directly in the first, fifth, and seventh movements and it is alluded to in arias nos. 2 and 4. While text for the cantata gives its own spin on the words of the *Magnificat*, Bach's music does the same with the melody that was in the minds of his listeners associated with this text. But it is not only the melody Bach works with. He also re-uses musical ideas from his magnificent Latin *Magnificat*: the introduction of the soprano as the first solo voice to speak the praise of Mary, the forceful bass solo meditating God's battle against the powerful rulers, and a love duet in which alto and tenor indulge harmoniously in divine love and mercy.

We do not know the sermon Bach's congregation would have heard after listening to the cantata on July 2, 1724. The preacher might have highlighted Mary as a model for humility, as does Luther in his writings on her.[20] He might also have talked about how God demonstrates his strength and power in everyday life; and he might have expounded on the idea that

God's mercy, which is mentioned twice in the text for the *Magnificat*, is rooted deeply in his love for mankind. All of these aspects Bach had already elaborated on in his "musical sermon."

Listeners who did not attend the morning service on July 2, 1724, the Feast of the Visitation, would have had an opportunity to hear the piece at the vespers service in the early afternoon. On this day in early July, however, the listeners might have encountered an unusual constellation. It is possible that Bach performed the *Magnificat* he had written for the very same feast one year prior. In that case, the congregation would actually have heard two *Magnificats*: the German cantata *Meine Seel' erhebt den Herren* towards the beginning of the service and the festive Latin *Magnificat* in its earlier version in E flat major. Some of them would have noticed the similarities between the two pieces: the staging of female humility, male power, and intimate love. This is only speculation, yet an intriguing one.

CHAPTER THREE

FROM LOVE SONG TO LULLABY
The *Christmas Oratorio* BWV 248

My heart, include this blessed marvel (BWV 248/31)

Johann Sebastian Bach did not compose operas. The primary reason for this is rather simple: he never was in the position to write one. He either held church positions where he did not have to compose secular stage works (as in Mühlhausen or Leipzig), or he worked at courts where regular opera performances were not common, as in Köthen and Weimar. Furthermore, in Leipzig—where he spent most of his life as cantor between 1723 and 1750—Bach arrived shortly after the public opera house had closed in 1720. Even though Bach did not compose operas himself, he was interested in this modern genre. We know that he attended opera performances in the Saxon capital, Dresden, and we can assume that he became acquainted with German baroque operas quite early in his career. However, in his position as cantor, composing operas was simply not part of his duties. It is futile to speculate whether Bach might have been a successful opera composer had he had the opportunity to write works for the stage. But it is clear that he was informed about what was going on in the world of opera in the 1720s and 1730s.[1]

This does not mean that he never attempted to write dramatic pieces in a broader sense. His large-scale passions, for instance, composed in 1724 and 1727, are highly dramatic. And in some of his cantatas we find dialogues, which also have a dramatic quality. But the proximity to contemporary opera is most palpable in a group of secular cantatas Bach composed in the early 1730s. He called these pieces *drammi per musica*, musical dramas, which was the contemporary term for a small-scale, opera-like composition.[2] The genesis of these secular cantatas, or *drammi per musica*, is instructive and it leads directly to the composition of the *Christmas Oratorio*.

In the early 1730s, Bach was dissatisfied with his position as cantor at St Thomas's in Leipzig, which he had held at this point for about a decade. He petitioned the electoral court in the Saxon capital, Dresden, to award him the prestigious title of "court composer." To that end, he composed at least eight cantatas for the court in Dresden between 1732 and 1735. Several of the cantatas (*drammi per musica*) use dialogues and allegorical or mythical characters, as we find frequently in baroque operas from the late seventeenth and early eighteenth centuries. The clearest example of an opera-like piece is the cantata *Laßt uns sorgen, laßt uns wachen* BWV 213 (Let us care for, let us watch), telling the story of the young Hercules at the crossroads, having to choose between vice and virtue. As with the other secular cantatas composed during the early 1730s, this one was only performed once, in September 1733, in one of the coffeehouses in Leipzig, one of the few places where secular music could be heard publicly in those days. The cantata was performed in honor of the birthday of the Crown Prince Friedrich Christian of Saxony. The author of the libretto was Christian Friedrich Henrici, called Picander (1700–1764), who probably furnished the libretto for the

Christmas Oratorio as well. As the music for the Hercules cantata had been written for a one-time event, it is understandable that Bach wanted the music to be used again. Given a new text and with some musical revisions, several of the movements from the secular *dramma per musica* found a new home in the *Christmas Oratorio*, composed in late 1734.

The genres of *dramma per musica* and oratorio are closely related. While the *dramma per musica* was the smaller relative of opera, the oratorio was the sacred sister of the genre. A contemporary music dictionary, edited by Johann Sebastian Bach's cousin Johann Gottfried Walther in 1732, provided a definition of "oratorio" that closely related it to opera:

> Oratorium . . . a sacred opera, or musical performance of a sacred historia in the chapels or chambers of great lords, consisting of dialogues, duos, trios, ritornellos, big choruses, etc. The musical composition must be rich in everything that art can muster in terms of ingenious and refined ideas.[3]

In other words, when Bach transferred movements from his *dramma per musica* to his oratorio, the movements stayed "in the family;" they remained within the realm of the opera-related genres, within the realm of dramatic music.

Altogether, nineteen of the sixty-four movements of the *Christmas Oratorio* were originally composed for other purposes (see Table 1 in Appendix B). We call the technique of recycling older musical material and providing it with a new text a parody. While it appeared esthetically suspicious to later generations, it was quite common among eighteenth-century composers. Bach's famous contemporaries George Frideric Handel and Johann Adolph Hasse used the technique repeatedly. In fact, Bach himself had already composed numerous parodies before he started writing his *Christmas Oratorio*. The newly composed material for the oratorio consisted of hymn settings, the settings of the biblical narrative, as well as one aria in part three and the opening chorus for part five.

Johann Sebastian Bach's autograph score for the oratorio is preserved in the German State Library (Deutsche Staatsbibliothek) in Berlin and it allows us fascinating insights into the compositional process.[4] The score immediately reveals which movements are parodies and which were newly conceived for the piece in 1734. The movements that were borrowed from the secular or sacred models are copied in neat and clear handwriting (figure 3.1). The newly composed sections, on the other hand, contain corrections, measures are crossed out; in one case (the alto aria in the third part, "Schließe, mein Herze"), Bach even began composing a movement, crossed out the measures and started all over with a completely new musical idea (figure 3.2).

Figure 3.1: Bach, *Christmas Oratorio* BWV 248/29, Duetto (autograph score, P 32, Deutsche Staatsbibliothek, Berlin, Musikabteilung/Mendelssohn-Archiv)

Figure 3.2: Bach, *Christmas Oratorio* BWV 248, draft for movement 31
"Schließe, mein Herze" (autograph score, P 32, Deutsche Staatsbibliothek,
Berlin, Musikabteilung/Mendelssohn-Archiv)

Lullaby and Love Song

Bach borrows most of the movements from the Hercules
cantata, *Laßt uns sorgen, laßt uns wachen* BWV 213, for the
Christmas Oratorio. The piece itself is almost a little operatic
scene: the young hero Hercules, while traveling through an
Arcadian landscape, arrives at a crossroads where he meets
two women (figure 3.3). One of them is the vice *Pleasure*
(Wollust), symbolizing lust and carnal desire, and the other
symbolizes *Virtue* (Tugend). Young Hercules hesitates for a

Figure 3.3: John Wierix, *Hercules at the Crossroads* (after Crispin van den Broeck (1524–91))

moment, unsure what to do. Should he follow his inborn proclivity for virtue or should he give in to his desires? Each of the two women tries to convince the young hero to follow her way. As can be expected, the vice attempts to seduce the hero. She tries to lull him into sleep with a beautifully seductive lullaby:

3. Aria (Pleasure, soprano)

Schlafe, mein Liebster, und pflege der Ruh,	Sleep, my dearest, and take your ease,
Folge der Lockung entbrannter Gedanken.	Follow the enticement of inflamed thoughts.
Schmecke die Lust	Taste the pleasure
Der lüsternen Brust,	Of the wanton breast,
Und erkenne keine Schranken.	And know no bounds.

Still, young Hercules is unsure. He asks the nymph *Echo* which path to take: follow *Virtue* or give in to the enticing promises of *Pleasure*. *Echo* gives Hercules an answer. However, echoes can only repeat what we have already said, and so the nymph confirms what Hercules had known all along, to follow his "inborn desire" for *Virtue*. Bach stages the dialogue between Hercules and the nymph (which is more an inner dialogue within Hercules between his desires for a virtuous life and carnal satisfaction) with echo-effects in the instruments as well as between two singers (example 3.1).

After the final "yes" has been sung by the echo, *Virtue* finally speaks up in the following recitative and aria. She reminds Hercules of his heritage and of his responsibilities and promises: "through me your lustre and gleam shall rise to perfection."[5] Hercules' decision is not an easy one. However, after further contemplation the young hero dismisses *Pleasure*:

Example 3.1: Bach, *Laßt uns sorgen* BWV 213/5, mm. 44–9

9. Aria (Hercules, alto)

Ich will dich nicht hören, ich will dich nicht wissen,	I will not listen to you, I will not acknowledge you,
Verworfene Wollust, ich kenne dich nicht.	Depraved Pleasure, I know you not.
Denn die Schlangen,	For the serpents
So mich wollten wiegend fangen,	That would seize me in my cradle
Hab ich schon lange zermalmet, zerrissen.	I have long since crushed and torn.

With *Pleasure* gone, the way is paved for Hercules and *Virtue*. Not only does Hercules choose a virtuous life, but he also becomes engaged to be married to *Virtue*. Appropriately, the two of them sing a beautiful love duet, which could easily have found its way into a contemporary opera:

11. Aria Duetto
Hercules (alto)

Ich bin deine,	I am yours,

Virtue (tenor)

Du bist meine,	You are mine,

Both

Küsse mich,	Kiss me,
Ich küsse dich.	I kiss you.
Wie Verlobte sich verbinden,	Just as the betrothed are united,
Wie die Lust, die sie empfinden,	Just like the desire they feel,
Treu und zart und eiferig,	Faithful and tender and ardent,
So bin ich.	So am I.

Bach musically stages the unification of the two lovers, and their constant kissing, with the two singers moving in harmonious parallel motion; and the two voices frequently overlap.

The two lovers are truly intertwined (example 3.2). This is one of the most enticing and erotic moments in all of Bach's music!

Bach transferred all five arias from the Hercules cantata into the *Christmas Oratorio* and also borrowed the opening movement from the secular work for the introductory chorus of part four. The echo-aria was integrated into the fourth part as a dialogue between the faithful soul and the Holy Spirit, while the aria "Auf meinen Flügeln sollst du schweben" (On my wings you shall hover) serves as a model for the second aria of part four. Hercules' harsh rejection of *Pleasure* finds a new place in part one of the oratorio and *Pleasure*'s lullaby becomes a lullaby for the little Jesus in the manger, while the highly eroticized love duet is transformed into a celebration of divine mercy, which I have already mentioned in Chapter Two.

Bach re-used the music, but he rearranged the order of movements, combined the notes with a new text, changed the instrumentation, transposed the music, and assigned parts to different singers. In short, he reworked the secular pieces to make them fit their new home in the *Christmas Oratorio*. Were Bach's listeners aware of the secular model? Most of them were probably not. Even though the cantata was performed in Leipzig, it only saw a single performance and anyone who had

Example 3.2: Bach, *Laßt uns sorgen* BWV 213/11, mm. 39–42

not been at that performance would not have had a chance to get to know the piece. However, the secular cantatas, and the Hercules piece in particular, are important for us to know, because Bach used these secular pieces for the music he created for the oratorio. And with only a few minor changes, he turned a secular love duet into a beautiful piece celebrating the love for Jesus and a lullaby sung by the vice *Pleasure* into a lullaby for the little baby Jesus in the manger.

The transformation was quite easy in the case of *Pleasure*'s lullaby. The original is a movement with a soothing rocking motion and an extremely long note on the word "schlafe" (sleep); the voice clearly rests on one single pitch. The author of the text for Bach's oratorio knew this text, and he knew the music. He writes a new text that captures the affect and the mood of the secular model. But now, instead of seducing, it becomes a lullaby for the baby Jesus in the manger:

Hercules cantata	*Christmas Oratorio*
Schlafe, mein Liebster, und pflege der Ruh,	Schlafe, mein Liebster, genieße der Ruh,
Folge der Lockung entbrannter Gedanken.	Wache nach diesem vor aller Gedeihen!
Schmecke die Lust	Labe die Brust,
Der lüsternen Brust	Empfinde die Lust,
Und erkenne keine Schranken.	Wo wir unser Herz erfreuen!

Sleep, my dearest, and take your ease,	Sleep, my dearest, enjoy your rest,
Follow the enticement of inflamed thoughts.	Awake after this for the flourishing of all.
Taste the pleasure	Refresh your breast,
Of the wanton breast	Feel the delight
And know no bounds.	Where we gladden our hearts.

According to baroque esthetics, music was able to express certain affects, or moods. And even though the purpose of the two versions of the aria is completely different, the mood is the same: both versions are a lullaby. The person being lulled into sleep is of secondary importance (at least for the music). The genesis of the lullaby "Schlafe, mein Liebster" implicitly raises the question of the ambivalent power of music. In the secular cantata, the lullaby is employed by the vice *Pleasure* to seduce the young hero, while in the *Christmas Oratorio* essentially the same notes serve as a cradle song for the newborn Jesus. Was music to be seen as a vice or a virtue? This question was the trigger for an ongoing dispute about the use of music in the liturgy that stretched from the time of the Reformation to the eighteenth century and that was often divided along the lines of orthodox Lutherans (who supported the use of music) and Pietists (who challenged it).[6] For a Christian in the Lutheran tradition, the answer was rather straightforward: the ethical character of music was not inherent to the music itself but to its use, as Luther had emphasized in his preface to Georg Rhau's *Symphoniae iucundae* (1538), one of the founding documents of a Lutheran theology of music. Music, according to Luther, was seen as part of the divine creation and thus was good; however, it could be employed in a way that contradicted the divine plan, in which case it had to be rejected. However, if used properly, the art was to be commended.[7] In other words, a lullaby like the above aria could be sung by vice and virtue alike. The context (and the text associated with it) determined its ethical impact, so that the seductive lullaby could indeed be transformed into a song of rest for the newborn Son of God.

The same is true for the love duet from the end of the Hercules cantata BWV 213. Hercules and *Virtue* get engaged

and begin to kiss. How can you turn this into a piece for a
sacred oratorio? Again, the question is not what the text says
exactly and what its purpose is in the context of the cantata. It
is the affect, the mood the music projects that is important:
harmony, affection, love. Thus, the duet is turned into a piece
about God's mercy, compassion, and love:

29. Duetto (soprano and bass)

Herr, dein Mitleid, dein Erbarmen	Lord, your compassion, your mercy
Tröstet uns und macht uns frei.	Comforts us and makes us free.
Deine holde Gunst und Liebe,	Your pleasing favor and love,
Deine wundersamen Triebe	Your wondrous desires
Machen deine Vatertreu	Make your Fatherly faithfulness
Wieder neu.	New again.

The transformation from love duet into a meditation of
divine love was aided by the fact that Christmas, in Bach's
time, was understood as a demonstration of divine love. The
coming of Christ into the world had its equivalent in his
coming into the human heart. Furthermore, Jesus' entering the
human heart was often metaphorically visualized as a spiritual
marriage. The important seventeenth-century theologian,
Johann Arndt (1555–1621), describes this coming of Christ as
a spiritual marriage in his *Books on True Christianity*, a volume
that was also in Bach's personal library:

Durch die geistliche Ehe und Vermählung geschiehet die Vereinigung des HErrn Christi mit der gläubigen Seele.	The unification of the Lord Christ with the faithful soul is caused by the spiritual marriage and wedding.

Wenn der Bräutigam kommt, so freuet sich die H. Seele, und giebt genaue und fleißige Achtung auf seine Gegenwart; denn durch seine fröhliche, Herz-erquickende und H. Ankunft vertreibet er die Finsterniß und die Nacht. Das Herz hat süsse Freude, es fliessen die Wasser der Andacht, die Seele schmelzet vor Liebe, der Geist freuet sich, die Affecten und Begierden werden inbrünstig, die Liebe wird entzündet, das Gemüth jauchzet, der Mund lobet und preiset, und thut Gelübde, und alle Kräfte der Seelen freuen sich in und wegen des Bräutigams. Sie freuet sich, sage ich, daß sie den gefunden hat, welcher sie liebet, und daß der sie zur Braut auf- und angenommen, welchen sie ehret.

O welche Liebe! O welch ein feuriges Verlangen! O welche liebreiche Gespräche! O wie ein keuscher Kuß, wann der H. Geist herab kommt, wann der Tröster überschattet, wann der Höchste erleuchtet, wann das Wort des Vatters da ist, die Weißheit redet, und die Liebe freundlich sie umfänget.[8]

When the bridegroom arrives, the holy soul (*Seele*) is happy and pays exact and diligent attention to his presence; for his joyful, heart-refreshing and holy arrival drives away darkness and night. The heart has sweet joy, the waters of devotion flow, the soul melts for love, the spirit is full of joy, the affects and desires turn fervent, the love is ignited, the soul (*Gemüt*) rejoices, the mouth praises and extols and utters vows, and all the powers of the soul (*Seele*) rejoice in and because of the bridegroom. She (the soul) is full of joy, so I say, because she has found the one who loves her and because he has taken her as a bride. She honors him.

O what love! O what burning desire! O what conversations full of love! O what a chaste kiss, when the Holy Spirit descends, when the consoler overshadows, when the highest illuminates, when the word of the father is there, when (it) talks truth and when love embraces her warmly.

The image of bride and bridegroom is derived from the *Song of Songs* in the Old Testament. The bridegroom in this beautiful love poem was, in the Christian tradition, often interpreted as Christ, with the bride as the faithful believer. This imagery has also left its mark on other movements of the *Christmas Oratorio*. The first recitative-aria pair in part one of the oratorio already invokes the arrival of the "most beloved bridegroom" (recitative 3) and encourages Zion (the church) to "hurry on, to love the bridegroom most ardently" (aria 4). Bach's *Christmas Oratorio* tells the story of the birth of Christ, but it tells it as a love story between God and mankind! I will return to this aspect shortly.

Liturgical Contexts

When Bach composed his *Christmas Oratorio* in 1734, it was the first time that he had called one of his pieces an "oratorio." Several other oratorios would follow in the coming years: an oratorio for Easter Sunday, an oratorio for Ascension Day; but the *Christmas Oratorio* was the first time Bach turned his attention to this "sacred sister of the opera." The motivation is again connected to the electoral court in Dresden. On Good Friday 1734, just a bit more than half a year earlier, the great opera composer, Johann Adolph Hasse (1699–1783), had performed his first oratorio in Dresden. *Il cantico de' tre fanciulli*, based on a libretto by Stefano Benedetto Pallavicino (1672–1742), tells the story of the three young men in the oven of fire from Daniel 3. Given Bach's interest in the musical developments in Dresden, it is only natural that he was enticed to try to compose an oratorio as well. However, he was faced with a problem: there was no place for a large-scale piece like that in the musical life of Leipzig. This was different with the passions, which were performed in a separate afternoon service that revolved around the setting of the passion of Christ. During Christmas time, a venue for such a performance did not exist. Therefore, Bach and his librettist decided to conceive of the piece in six separate sections, each to be performed in one of the worship services in Leipzig on the three days of Christmas, New Year's Day, the Sunday after New Year's, and on the feast of Epiphany. The solution Bach found was elegant but not revolutionary. We find a similar separation of larger-scale works (especially passions) in other German churches during Bach's time. But it was a way for the Leipzig composer to write a large-scale oratorio and to perform it in the course of the regular worship services at Christmas time.

The liturgical function of the six parts explains the unusual structure of the oratorio. Instead of a continuous narrative, we have six self-contained sections, formally resembling Bach's regular church cantatas. Each section is framed by a large-scale introductory movement (mostly choral movements) and a final hymn setting. Within this framework, Bach and his librettist alternate between biblical narrative (mostly composed in simple, declamatory secco recitatives), arias and accompanied recitatives, which reflect on the biblical texts and interpret them for the individual believer, and settings of familiar hymns, which represent the view of the congregation and interpret the biblical narrative from their perspective.

The structure of each of the parts is straightforward: a section from the Christmas story is presented by the tenor (sometimes joined by other singers) and it is then interpreted in arias and hymns, which focus on the questions that preachers of the time asked in their sermons: "What does this mean for me?" and "How do I have to act?" In this structure lies one of the major differences between the oratorio and its secular relative, the opera. In an opera the recitatives drive the action forward in dialogues between the protagonists on stage. Conversely, the arias, sung by the same actors, reflect on the emotional impact of the events. In the *Christmas Oratorio* the "action" is not staged but only reported in the recitatives and the events are subsequently interpreted by other singers, who are in time and space separated from the biblical narrative.

A sequence of movements from part three can serve as an example of this hermeneutic practice. The biblical text narrates that Mary, the mother of Jesus, kept all the words she had heard from the shepherds in her heart. The following alto aria reflects on this from the perspective of the individual believer, who will herself, in turn, keep these words in her heart:

31. Aria (alto)

Schließe, mein Herze, dies selige Wunder	My heart, include this blessed marvel
Fest in deinem Glauben ein!	Steadfastly in your faith!
Lasse dies Wunder, die göttlichen Werke,	Let this marvel, the Godly deeds,
Immer zur Stärke	Be ever at hand for the strengthening
Deines schwachen Glaubens sein!	Of your weak faith!

Following the aria, a short recitative—sung by the alto as well—confirms that she (Mary) wants to keep these words in her heart. The opening phrase of the recitative, "Mein Herz soll es bewahren" (My heart shall safeguard) directly prepares the entrance of the following hymn stanza, which represents the voice of the congregation, "Ich will dich mit Fleiß bewahren" (I will safeguard you with diligence). We see how biblical narrative and individual and communal reflection are interwoven into a complex interpretative fabric. Bach's librettist uses common keywords to connect the movements thematically:

Gospel (no. 30)	Mary *kept* all these words . . . in her *heart*
Aria (no. 31)	My *heart* shall *safeguard*
Recit. (no. 32)	Yes, yes, my *heart* shall *safeguard*
Chorale (no. 33)	I will *safeguard* you

Two Narratives

Not only is Christ, the word incarnate, to be kept and safeguarded, but he is to dwell in the human heart. The seventeenth-century poet and mystic Angelus Silesius (1624–1677) summarizes this common understanding of Christmas in the late seventeenth and early eighteenth centuries in the following aphorism: *If Christ had been born a thousand times in Bethlehem, but not in you, you would be lost forever.* Christmas, which celebrated the incarnation of Christ, could only be fully understood if its meaning in the lives of individuals was made apparent. As I have mentioned earlier, the *Christmas Oratorio* tells the story of Christ's incarnation as a love story between God and mankind. It is the story of Christ (as the divine word incarnate) entering and dwelling in the human heart. This arrival of Christ in the heart is told as a process throughout the oratorio. The first part of the oratorio announces the coming of Christ, the bridegroom, and the final hymn of that part asks Christ to make the heart a cradle and a dwelling place for himself as the Son of God:

9. Chorale

Ach mein herzliebes Jesulein,	Oh my beloved little Jesus,
Mach dir ein rein sanft Bettelein,	Make for yourself a perfectly soft little bed,
Zu ruhn in meines Herzens Schrein,	To rest in the shrine of my heart,
Dass ich nimmer vergesse dein!	That I may never forget you!

The aria "Schließe, mein Herze" (see above) from part three admonishes the human heart to embrace Jesus, and the terzetto from part five of the oratorio finally proclaims: "He is already here!" (no. 51). And it is because of Jesus' presence in the heart that the final part of the *Christmas Oratorio* can look ahead to the end of times and can proclaim the victory over "death, devil, sin, and hell" in the final chorale:

64. Chorale

Nun seid ihr wohl gerochen	Now you all are well avenged
An eurer Feinde Schar,	Of your band of enemies,
Denn Christus hat zerbrochen,	For Christ has broken apart
Was euch zuwider war.	What was against you.
Tod, Teufel, Sünd und Hölle	Death, devil, sin, and hell
Sind ganz und gar geschwächt;	Are completely diminished;
Bei Gott hat seine Stelle	The human race
Das menschliche Geschlecht.	Has its place by God.

Within the narrative logic of the *Christmas Oratorio*, the historical event of Christ's birth, his present coming into the believer's heart, and his victorious return at the end of time are intrinsically intertwined. This reflects the doctrine of the "Threefold Advent of Christ" as it was taught by theologians and preachers in Bach's time. Hamburg theologian Johann Joachim Neudorf (169?–1752), in a book for schoolchildren from 1727, traces the three steps of Christ's coming. Bach's listeners would have recognized the three steps in the libretto of the oratorio. Neudorf differentiates between the three modes of Christ's coming ("Zukunft Christi"):

1. Ins Fleisch, (oder zu unserer Erlösung,) die ist vergangen.	1. Into the flesh (or for our salvation); this one has passed.

2. In unsere Hertzen, (zu unserer   2. Into our hearts (for our
   Heiligung,) die ist gegenwärtig,   sanctification); this one is the
   (oder geschieht täglich.)   present [mode] (or happens
                                               daily).

3. Zum Gericht, die ist zukünftig.[9]   3. For the [Final] Judgment; this
                                               one lies in the future.

Now that we have identified the underlying theological framework of the oratorio, we shall look at the six parts in more detail.

Part I

The first part was performed on the first day of Christmas,
December 25, 1734. The opening movement, "Jauchzet, froh-
locket, auf preiset die Tage" (Shout, exult, arise, praise the days)
serves, with its celebratory character, as a portal to the entire
oratorio. Bach borrowed the movement almost without any
changes from the secular cantata *Tönet, ihr Pauken! Erschallet,
Trompeten* BWV 214 (Sound, you drums! Ring out, you trumpets!). Here in the secular cantata, the instrumentation—with
trumpets and timpani—directly depicts the words of the text:
the movement begins with four beats of the timpani, then the
flutes enter with a short motive, next the oboes, and then the
first trumpet plays a festive fanfare. The sound gradually
expands while the different groups of instruments are introduced. When Bach borrowed the movement for the *Christmas
Oratorio*, the instrumentation lost its close correlation with the
text; however, the gradual expansion of sound, culminating in
the royal fanfare of the trumpets, still underscores the celebratory character of the day (example 3.3).

After a section of the biblical narrative and a short recitative, the alto sings an aria that was originally sung by Hercules
to drive away the vice *Pleasure*:

9. Aria (Hercules, alto)

Ich will dich nicht hören, ich will dich nicht wissen,	I will not listen to you, I will not acknowledge you,
Verworfene Wollust, ich kenne dich nicht.	Depraved Pleasure, I know you not.

The original setting underscores the stubborn character of the words: the piercing sound of the strings, which play short, detached staccato notes. The text in the sacred parody has the opposite affect:

4. Aria (alto)

Bereite dich, Zion, mit zärtlichen Trieben,	Make yourself ready, Zion, with tender desires,
Den Schönsten, den Liebsten bald bei dir zu sehn!	To see the Most Handsome, the Most Beloved, soon at your side!

How could Bach decide to use the old music with the new text? The emotions conveyed could not be more contrary. With a few adjustments, however, the composer changes the

Example 3.3: Bach, *Christmas Oratorio* BWV 248/1, mm. 1–5

character completely. The piercing sound of the strings in the original are replaced with oboi d'amore, or "love oboes," which produce a much smoother sound. Furthermore, Bach replaces the staccato—the short, detached notes played by the instruments—with a soothing legato line. Only a few more changes in the part of the singer were necessary to make the listener forget about the original words and turn a stubborn rejection of vice into a song welcoming Christ, the beloved bridegroom.

The next sequence of movements elaborates on the paradox of Christ's birth: how could God's son be born as a poor child? Eighteenth-century theologians point out that this paradox is incomprehensible for the human mind. Johann Christoph Wenzel (1659–1732), a poet and teacher at the school in Zittau (about 120 miles east of Leipzig), summarizes this paradox nicely in a school play, performed by the boys of his school in 1718. The character Reason (Ratio) approaches the manger. He carries a modern technical device, a telescope, as a symbol for his scientific approach; however, he refuses to accept that the unassuming child could be the son of God:

[...] tritt Ratio auf und siehet mit einem Fern-Glaß nach der Krippe und Kinde JEsu/ gestehet aber/ daß sie sich nimmermehr überreden werde/ das unansehnliche Kind vor Gottes Sohn zu erkennen.[10]	[...] enter Ratio searching with a telescope for the manger and the child Jesus; however, he confesses that he will never be persuaded to accept the shabby child as the Son of God.

How can music capture the incomprehensible? Bach chooses an interesting way of setting the text. He composes a dialogue between a bass voice and the soprano. The bass expresses his doubts, and questions how the incarnation could be understood; the soprano answers with lines from the hymn, "Er ist auf Erden kommen arm" (He has come on earth poor). As mentioned earlier, the hymns represent the voice of the church, and the soprano states the position of the church: God had to become poor in order to save mankind. Throughout the dialogue the bass grows more and more confident until he can finally answer with the following aria, "Großer Herr, o starker König" (Great Lord, o mighty King). The bass, representing the voice of the individual believer, has finally understood that God reveals himself as king through the poverty of the poor child in the manger. What seemed to be an insurmountable dichotomy is now understood as two sides of the same coin.

The final hymn setting of part one, sung by the entire ensemble, confirms this, and Bach's composition again reflects the dichotomy between God's poverty and his regal character. The text of the hymn states: "O my beloved little Jesus, make for yourself a perfectly soft little bed, to rest in the shrine of my heart, that I may never forget you." The lines of this song to the sweet little Jesus are interrupted with interludes by the trumpets, the instrument commonly associated with royalty. By juxtaposing these contrasting sonic spheres Bach again epitomizes the paradox of Christ's incarnation. The little movement fulfills two other functions: the instrumentation is the same as in the first movement and Bach uses it to balance the two framing sections of the first part of the oratorio. The third function is of a theological nature; it is the summary of what Christmas (in Bach's time) is all about: the coming of Christ into the human heart, which is here metaphorically imagined as a manger.

Part II

The recurring theme of the second part of the *Christmas Oratorio* is the power of music: towards the end of part two, the angels sing their praise of God in their chorus, "Ehre sei Gott in der Höhe" (May honor be to God on high) and thus set a model for human music, which should mirror the sounds of the heavenly realm. The lullaby "Schlafe, mein Liebster" (Sleep, my dearest) (no. 19), uses music to lull the baby Jesus to sleep; and the final chorale of part two confidently confirms that humans and angels are united in one chorus in their praise of Christ: "Wir singen dir in deinem Heer" (We sing to you, amid your host).

The unique power of music is even more prominent in the opening movement for part two. Instead of an opening chorus, Bach composes a purely instrumental sinfonia. Compared to the regal sounds of the trumpets in part one, it now takes the listener into a different sonic sphere: Bach writes a dialogue between the strings and flutes of the orchestra and the nasal sound of the oboes. He paints a bucolic scene: a sonic image that shows the shepherds in the fields, encountering the angels from above. The composer uses two distinct groups of instruments to depict the angels (represented by the strings and flutes) and the shepherds (represented by the oboes). Bach employs conventional stereotypes to denote the two spheres. The nasal sound of the oboes had been associated with the shepherds since the Middle Ages, and we find numerous paintings, especially in the Renaissance, which show the shepherds with similar instruments.

The sinfonia evokes a bucolic scene, not unlike a shepherd's scene in a contemporary opera, but it also foreshadows the interaction between the shepherds and the angels. At the beginning, the two instrumental groups are separated. But throughout the movement, the earthly and heavenly orchestras repeatedly play together, and in the final measures they are eventually united when the oboes (shepherds) take over the musical motive from the strings (angels). The unification of celestial and mundane (earthly) choirs, which the closing chorale for part two mentions, is already realized musically in the opening movement.

The following movements again provide several sequences of biblical texts and interpretations through arias and hymns. A musical highlight is the beautiful lullaby, sung by the alto, "Schlafe, mein Liebster, genieße der Ruh" (Sleep, my dearest, enjoy your rest). I mentioned this movement earlier. The second part of the oratorio reaches its climax in the choir of the angels: "Glory to God on high." The movement reveals again Bach's sense for musical drama. All other parts of the *Christmas Oratorio* begin with a festive, large-scale choral movement. He could have begun this part with a similar piece. Instead, he composes the quiet instrumental sinfonia and reserves the entrance of the full chorus for the praise of the angels, which increases the impact of this movement when it finally sounds.

Part III

Bach employs a different framework in the third part of the oratorio, originally performed on the third day of Christmas. This part is opened by a short yet festive movement, "Ruler of Heaven, give heed to our babble," a piece originally composed for the secular cantata *Tönet, ihr Pauken* BWV 214. Since the movement is rather brief, Bach repeats the movement at the end. The biblical narrative that follows reports the departure of the angels and tells how the shepherds decide to go to Bethlehem. Bach sets the text, "Let us go to Bethlehem and see the story," as a fugue: one voice follows the other and we can almost see how the shepherds, one after the other, depart for the manger.

The two large solo movements of part three center on the coming of Christ into the human heart and on the love between Christ and the believer. The first aria is the beautiful duet for soprano and bass that Bach had borrowed from the love duet in the Hercules cantata BWV 213. The aria's position within the drama of the oratorio is of utmost importance. This is because the "love duet" is a reaction to the choir of the angels. In other words, the answer to the message that Jesus is born is a confession of love. It is the spiritual love between Christ and the believer. The second aria of part three is the only one that was originally composed for the *Christmas Oratorio*. It is the alto aria "Schließe, mein Herze," which highlights the coming of Christ (his second coming) into the human heart through the word of God. I have discussed how this aria transforms the biblical image of Mary keeping the words in her heart, into a promise by the believer to safeguard the word in her heart as well.

Part IV

The last three parts of the oratorio were performed between New Year and Epiphany 1735; they narrate the events after Christ's birth: his circumcision and naming, and the adoration of the three wise men. The text for the oratorio continues to elaborate on the understanding of Christmas as a feast of love between Christ, the bridegroom, and the believer, his bride. This theology of love is most central in the fourth part, composed for New Year's Day 1735.

In order to appreciate Bach's composition, we have to have a look at the contemporary understanding of this day. New Year's Day had two meanings in the seventeenth and eighteenth centuries. Firstly, it marked the beginning of the secular year, beginning with January 1. Indeed we find references to the secular character of the feast in Bach's previously composed cantatas for this occasion: prayers for the authorities, the government, and the city as well as for Church and schools. On two occasions, Bach even quotes from the German *Te Deum*, a hymn of thanksgiving that was closely associated with secular celebrations, such as victories, coronations, or the praise of the authorities in general, in the baroque.[11] Bach was clearly familiar with the secular side of the day. But the day had a religious significance as well. It was the feast of the circumcision of Jesus[12] and the day when he, according to the tradition of the church, received his name. New Year's Day was therefore also celebrated as the day of the name of Jesus. Most of Bach's cantatas for January first mention both sides of the day, the secular and the religious. The balance shifts to one side or the other, but both of them are usually present.

The fourth part of the *Christmas Oratorio* breaks with this rule. Since the oratorio is a dramatization and an interpretation of the nativity story from the New Testament, there is no room for the secular side of the feast or intercessions for the government. We can assume that these found their place at other points of the liturgy on January 1, 1735, but we do not find them in the oratorio. This is not because Bach rejected the secular side (later cantata performances present again a balance between the two meanings of the day), but rather because it did not fit into the overall dramatic and theological concept of the piece.

However, even without its secular connotations, New Year's Day still is an occasion for praise and thanksgiving and so the fourth part of the oratorio is opened by a festive movement for choir and orchestra, "Fallt mit Danken, fallt mit Loben" (Bow with thanksgiving, bow with lauding). It represents a universal praise of Christ as the redeemer of mankind. The movement was originally composed for the Hercules cantata from 1733, where it is the first movement. There, it serves as a chorus of the pagan gods who decide to protect and support their son, Hercules. The two texts, the secular and the sacred, exhibit some interesting connections and it is obvious that the author of the libretto for the oratorio used the secular text as a point of departure. The original text reads: "Let us care for, let us watch over our divine son, our throne will on earth become glorious and radiant." This is turned into: "Bow with thanksgiving, bow with lauding before the Most High's Throne of Grace. God's son is willing to become the earth's Savior and redeemer." Both texts mention the throne—even though in different contexts—and the divine son Hercules from the secular cantata now becomes the Son of God. In German, this connection is even more obvious: Göttersohn–Gottes Sohn.

The next movement is a short recitative, presenting the only biblical text of the entire fourth part: "And as eight days were up, when the child would be circumcised, his name was called Jesus, [the name he] was called by the angel, before he was conceived in the womb."[13] All the following movements are an extensive meditation on the meaning and significance of the name of Jesus. The first step in the interpretation of the verse from the Gospel of Luke is a sequence of three movements forming a unity: two recitatives juxtaposing bass and soprano, which frame the echo-aria for soprano.

The two recitatives (nos. 38 and 40) combine a declamatory part in the bass voice with the text of a congregational hymn. Interestingly, Bach only uses the text, not the melody that was associated with the words. He creates a new melody instead. The voice leading of the chorale melody is much closer to the emotional tone of the baroque song-aria than a traditional hymn. This seems to be appropriate in light of the highly emotional text. The two voices sound like a love duet—"Jesus, you, my most beloved life, my soul's bridegroom" and "Come! with delight I will embrace you, my heart shall never leave you." Bach's music underscores this "lovin' feeling:" in its first phrase, the soprano voice outlines a beautiful F major chord, and the melody is accompanied by the two violins in parallel thirds, a feature that is often found in love duets of the time to signify unity and harmony. Even the bass and soprano move frequently in these consonant thirds (example 3.4).

The movement is followed by an aria, which is again a parody; it is based on the echo-aria from the Hercules cantata. The original text is a dialogue between the hero and the nymph *Echo*. In the parody, the aria is turned into an intimate dialogue between the believer and an echo, which can be understood as the voice of the Holy Spirit (or Christ) in the human heart. Interestingly, we find visual images in the seventeenth century in Germany that depict the dialogue between Christ and the individual as an echo (figure 3.4). While the echo-aria might sound unusual to some modern listeners, the concept we find in Bach's aria was quite familiar to his contemporaries.

The three movements, the two recitatives combined with the chorale, and the aria, evoke images of the deepest connection between the faithful and Jesus. The following aria, sung by the tenor, draws the consequences from this intimate relationship: "Ich will nur dir zu Ehren leben" (For honor I will live only for you). The emotional proximity between the human

Example 3.4: Bach, *Christmas Oratorio* BWV 248/38, mm. 10–12

and the divine leads to a self-commitment on behalf of the
believer.

The fourth part ends with another compositional experi-
ment by Bach. He had already abandoned the original hymn
tune in the recitatives, and created his own melody. He does the
same in a setting that only stylistically resembles the last movements of earlier cantatas. The hymn text is presented line by
line in a simple four-part setting, interrupted by instrumental
interludes. The only difference is that Bach now composes his
own melody, just pretending to write a hymn setting. The

Figure 3.4: Heinrich Müller, *Geistlicher Danck-Altar*, Frankfurt/M 1700 (Sächsische Landes- und Universitätsbibliothek, Dresden/Digitale Sammlungen, Theol.ev.asc.1506)

reason is that the melodies that were associated with this text were all in a dark, minor tonality, but Bach needed a melody that was in bright major—and so he wrote his own tune.

Parts V and VI

The last two parts of the *Christmas Oratorio* tell the story of the three wise men who follow the star in search of the manger. While the fourth part of the oratorio was highly experimental, the following two parts are much more conventional. Both are opened by large-scale introductory movements and end with a chorale setting, which uses the traditional melodies. However, the two parts are peculiar in another way. The gospel for the Sunday after New Year, for which the fifth part was intended, is the flight to Egypt, while the gospel on Epiphany is the arrival and the adoration of the three wise men. The gospel texts are not in chronological order. As gospel readings for two different days this does not pose a problem. However, in a dramatic context like the oratorio, which tries to keep the chronology of the events intact, it is. It would not make sense to send Jesus, Mary, and Joseph on January 2 to Egypt and then four days later have them back at the manger welcoming the wise men. Bach and his librettist had two choices: they could either rearrange the gospels, which would have been a problem since the original gospel readings would still have appeared in the liturgy immediately before the piece, or they could skip the flight to Egypt and split the story about the three wise men into two parts, the first half to be performed on the Sunday after New Year and the second half on the feast of Epiphany. They chose the latter alternative.

The fifth part narrates the arrival of the wise men and the conspiring of King Herod to use them as spies to find the newborn Jesus. The entire piece revolves around the juxtaposition of light and darkness—the light of the star that guided the travelers to Bethlehem and the darkness of the plans of the king. But it is also the light of Christ and the darkness of the sinfulness of the human soul, or in the metaphor prevalent in the *Christmas Oratorio*, the human heart. Everything leads again to the idea of Christ dwelling in the believer's heart. But the libretto is realistic: the last movement of the fifth part states:

53. Chorale

Zwar ist solche Herzensstube	True, such a heart-cellar
Wohl kein schöner Fürstensaal,	Is certainly no choice hall of princes
Sondern eine finstre Grube;	But rather a dark pit;
Doch, sobald dein Gnadenstrahl	Yet, as soon as your grace-filled stream of light
In denselben nur wird blinken,	Flashes into the same [cellar],
Wird es voller Sonnen dünken.	It will seem full of sunlight.

One of the movements of part five that poses a problem for us musicologists is the terzetto for soprano, alto, and tenor, "Ach, wenn wird die Zeit erscheinen?" (Oh, when will the time appear?). The movement sonically stages a conversation between two characters with doubts about the coming of Christ (sung by soprano and tenor) and the alto, representing the confident believer, who reiterates that Christ is already present.

There is no parody model for this movement and it is not part of any of the secular cantatas Bach used as a basis for his *Christmas Oratorio*. We would normally assume that the terzetto was an original composition. However, as I mentioned earlier, it is generally easy to differentiate between original compositions and parodies in Bach's score because the first show numerous corrections while the latter are mostly written in clear, neat handwriting. The terzetto is written quite neatly, suggesting that it was borrowed from an earlier cantata. We therefore have to assume that the movement had its origins in an earlier, probably secular cantata, that is now lost. When listening to the piece, it is easy to imagine that it was a trio from a secular piece like the Hercules cantata. The text must have featured three protagonists—perhaps gods from Greek or Roman mythology or ancient heroes like Hercules.

The three voices in Bach's terzetto are engaged in conversation. Soprano and tenor mostly move in close harmony, often in parallel motion. The two singers concur in their questioning when the time of Christ's arrival might occur. When will he come? When will he save his people? Only after these questions have been posed does the alto enter the musical stage. The singer's musical material is different from that used by soprano and tenor. Her first word is "silence" and she continues, "he really is already here!" The two other singers continue their questions, but at the end of each musical phrase (and consequently at the very end of the terzetto), the alto has the last word: He is already here. The bridegroom has arrived in the heart of the bride (example 3.5).

Bach's *Christmas Oratorio* ends with a composition for the Feast of Epiphany on January 6, 1735. It is the only part of the *Christmas Oratorio* that is not directly based on earlier secular pieces; instead scholars have been able to show that most of the movements were actually taken in their entirety from an earlier sacred cantata. It is the first time since the third day of Christmas, on December 27, that we hear

Example 3.5: Bach, *Christmas Oratorio* BWV 248/51, mm. 166–70

trumpets and drums. The royal instruments appear in the opening movement for part six and return in the closing chorale for a festive and celebratory finale to the oratorio. The last part of the oratorio shows Bach's sense of balance and symmetrical structure that we have already observed on a micro-level in several parts of the oratorio. He now balances the beginning and the end of the entire large-scale oratorio. And he also returns to the initial key of D major, which opened the composition.

In the doctrine of the "Threefold Advent of Christ," the first coming is the historical coming, the second his arrival in the human heart, and the third is his return at the end of time for the eschatological battle and the salvation of mankind.

Since the terzetto in part five had proclaimed that "He" was already there, the last part of the *Christmas Oratorio* now addresses the third coming. The text for part six talks about the enemies of Christ. It refers foremost to King Herod, who threatens the life of the baby Jesus; but, in a broader sense, the text also refers to the enemies of the believers in general. Some scholars have described the opening movement as a musical battle scene, a term that captures quite well the tumultuous texture of the instrumental parts and the battle fanfares by the trumpet. It reflects the text, which invokes God's support and protection against the "snorting" of the "insolent enemies."

The second aria, a movement for tenor, draws a connection between the love imagery of earlier parts of the oratorio and the fight against these adversaries:

62. Aria (tenor)

Nun mögt ihr stolzen Feinde schrecken;	Now you insolent enemies might horrify;
Was könnt ihr mir für Furcht erwecken?	[Yet] how could you arouse any fear in me?
Mein Schatz, mein Hort ist hier bei mir.	My treasure, my refuge is here with me.
Ihr mögt euch noch so grimmig stellen,	You do still so like to feign being fierce,
Droht nur, mich ganz und gar zu fällen,	Just [go ahead and] threaten to bring me down completely,
Doch seht! mein Heiland wohnet hier.	But look! my Savior dwells here.

The "here" that denotes the Savior's dwelling place is, in accordance with the theology of the *Christmas Oratorio*, the heart of the faithful believer.

Dramatic Unity

The *Christmas Oratorio* consists of six independent parts, each performed on a different day and each designed for the liturgical requirements of a different day of the Christmas season; and yet, the six pieces also form a unity—the narrative follows a logical chronological order. The piece also returns sonically and tonally to the beginning. And it has a coherent theology that traces the coming of Christ from the historical events in Bethlehem to his coming into the believer's heart, to his return at the end of time. Bach understood this and conceived of the six parts as a unity.

This brings us back to the beginning of this essay. In the early 1730s, Bach was fascinated by operas staged in Dresden and he was interested in the composition of large-scale pieces that went beyond the liturgical restrictions of the church cantata he could perform during the liturgy and which lasted only about twenty to thirty minutes. In the case of the *Christmas Oratorio*, he found a viable solution that would satisfy his own fascination with dramatic music and keep within the constraints of the liturgy.

Several of the pieces that Bach "recycled" for the *Christmas Oratorio* were "love songs," arias that talked about love, harmonious duets that celebrated the harmony between two lovers. Bach's *Christmas Oratorio* tells the story of Christmas and dramatically stages some parts of this narrative. But it does more than that. It interprets the Christmas story from a very individual perspective as an act of divine love. Jesus is the bridegroom, the most beloved; he dwells in the human heart. The *Christmas Oratorio* is a celebratory piece—who could deny that after the majestic opening movement?—but it is also a very intimate piece. And this intimacy correlates with

the use of the secular models. Since the text for the oratorio
borrows metaphors from the field of human love—such as
bridegroom and beloved—Bach could transform movements
that had expressed the desire for a lover in his secular cantatas
into meditations on the desire for the presence of the divine in
the human heart.

CHAPTER FOUR

DIVINE GLORY AND HUMAN SUFFERING

The *St John Passion* BWV 245

Even in the greatest humiliation you have been glorified
(BWV 245/1)

Let me begin with two meditations on the passion of Christ.

O most beloved wounds of my Lord Jesus Christ! For when I entered into them somehow with eyes open, those eyes were filled with blood, so that, able to see nothing else, I began to proceed, reaching with my hands until I came to the inmost substance of his charity, and once embraced on all sides, I could not turn back. And for that reason I live there, and with what food he is fed, I am fed, and I am intoxicated with his drink.[1]

Another text, written about 400 years later:

My heart—while the entire world with Jesus' suffering likewise suffers, the sun clothes itself in mourning, the veil tears, the rock crumbles, the earth quakes, the graves split open, because they see the creator growing cold—what will you do for your part?—Dissolve, my heart, in floods of tears to honor the Most High! Declare to the world and to Heaven the distress: your Jesus is dead![2]

The two texts, one by the thirteenth-century Franciscan theologian James of Milan and the other one from Johann Sebastian Bach's *St John Passion*, were written almost half a millennium apart and reflect quite different theological traditions. However, the texts exhibit a similar approach to the meaning of the passion of Christ. This meaning is not accessible to the passive bystander; the faithful believer has to enter the narrative herself to appreciate its significance. James of Milan enters the wounds of Christ, is drenched in his blood and touches the substance of his charity. In the piece from Bach's passion, the believer's heart dissolves in tears when she beholds how Christ gave up his life. The passion of Christ creates, to borrow a term from Barbara Rosenwein, an *Emotional Community*.[3] It is a community including the suffering Son of God; but it is also a community with others who behold that suffering. The individual, while responding to the death of Christ, is also at the same time part of the larger church, the Community of Saints, as the Creed calls it. Here again, the medieval tradition and the text of Bach's passion intersect.

The proper way of beholding and of "entering" the passion narrative at the core of both Bach's *St John Passion* and his later *St Matthew Passion* is encapsulated in an image that appeared in print contemporaneous to the composer's completion of his two passion settings. In 1724, the theologian Abraham Wiegner published a book with the Leipzig publisher Johann Christian Martini with the title *Nöthige Freytags-Arbeit* (Necessary Occupation on a Friday). It belongs to the popular genre of passion meditations that appeared in print in the seventeenth and early eighteenth centuries. The book provides the reader with a variety of material to contemplate the death of Christ at home: the biblical narrative is broken up into sections; each chapter begins with a part of the biblical story, presented in the version from Johann Bugenhagen's *Passion Harmony*, which is a compilation of the passion narratives from the four gospels. The passion harmony was quite popular in Lutheran Germany at that time. Even the sermon in the afternoon service on Good Friday in Leipzig, the vespers, was based on this compilation of the events. In Wiegner's book, each section of the biblical narrative is followed by meditative texts on the events of Christ's passion, accompanied by hymns that made the meditative reflections singable. Additionally, Wiegner illuminated the texts with fifty-two engravings depicting the scenes from the passion of Christ. While most of these engravings are more or less naturalistic depictions of the biblical narrative, the first image is different (figure 4.1). We see Jesus at the cross with the familiar paraphernalia of the passion story: the rooster which reminded Peter of his betrayal;

Figure 4.1: Abraham Wiegner, *Nöthige Freytags-Arbeit* (Leipzig, 1724), 1 (Bayerische Staatsbibliothek, Munich)

the sponge on a stick that had been used to give Jesus vinegar to drink; the three dice the soldiers had thrown to determine who would win Jesus' cloak.

In the foreground, we see a figure that is not part of the passion story. It is a woman in a long dress. She wears an amulet showing Christ crucified; flames surround her heart. A *subscriptio* explains: "My heart shall burn for God. Leave behind what is futile. Only the Crucified can refresh the dull spirit."[4] The woman in the engraving represents the faithful believer. She is clearly not a part of the narrative. She is not even part of Jesus' time. She becomes part of the story by beholding and meditating on the suffering of Christ. The woman carries the crucified in her heart; a heart that burns with desire and compassion for Jesus. The believer, this woman in the picture, is removed from the historical events in time and space. But through her meditations and by carrying the crucified in her heart, she becomes a beholder of the events— not much different from James of Milan, who entered the wounds of Christ. I will return later to this image and to the concept of passion meditation it represents. What is interesting for now is that the book and the images were published in the same year Bach performed his *St John Passion* for the first time. The listeners at the performance on Good Friday 1724 could have left the church and gone home to read the meditations in Wiegner's book, or they could have looked at the images while Bach's music still lingered in their memories!

There is no evidence, of course, that this really happened. And likewise, we do not know whether Bach was aware of the book. However, the local and chronological proximity allows us to employ the images of the book as a visual commentary on the events of Christ's passion. The first image in particular serves as a hermeneutic key for how to understand meditative texts in Bach's passions. But before we delve into the details of Bach's work, it is necessary to provide some historical background information.

Versions and Revisions

According to the estate catalogue compiled by his son Carl Philipp Emanuel, Johann Sebastian Bach composed five passions. The passions according to John and Matthew are two of the best-known works and most performed large-scale compositions by Bach. Furthermore, he composed passion settings based on the Evangelists Mark and Luke.[5] The *St Mark Passion* BWV 247 is mostly lost. The recitatives and hymn settings are missing, while the music for arias and some of the choral movements exist, as they were parodied from works with different texts. The passion can be partly reconstructed but there is always a degree of uncertainty about whether this is really Bach or just our idea of what Bach should sound like. The *St Luke Passion*, on the other hand, is completely lost. There exists a passion based on the Gospel of Luke that was for a long time attributed to Bach, but scholars today agree that the piece was not composed by him. The fifth composition, mentioned by Carl Philipp Emanuel Bach, was composed during Bach's time in Weimar and it was performed at the court in Gotha in 1717. While we are informed about the piece because Bach was paid for the performance, more than just this mention in the Gotha court records is not known. It is possible that movements from this early work were re-used in later passions, such as the *St John Passion*, but there is no further evidence for that.

While there is scant material for these three lesser-known passions, we are faced with an overabundance of sources for the

St John Passion. The piece has a long history of versions and revisions.[6] The first version of the passion was performed in the afternoon vespers of Good Friday 1724, in St Nicholas in Leipzig. In the following year, Bach returned to this composition and reworked it for another performance.[7] Further revisions followed for performances around 1730 and towards the end of Bach's life in 1749. To make things more complicated, Bach also worked on a revised score around 1739, which was not connected to a performance and which he soon abandoned.[8]

While the first version from 1724 and the later versions from the 1730s and 1740s are quite similar (the differences lie in some text changes and some smaller revisions of the music), the version from 1725 differs quite significantly from its predecessor.[9] Bach composed a completely new opening movement and replaced some of the arias. The changes he made are significant for his own artistic development during the year 1724/5 and reflect his interest in settings of Protestant hymns during summer, fall, and winter 1724. We have seen one of these so-called chorale cantatas in Chapter Two, Bach's German version of the Song of Mary, *Meine Seel' erhebt den Herren* BWV 10.

The version of the *St John Passion* that is most commonly performed today is an amalgamation of the earliest and later versions. In other words, it is a modern reconstruction; but a reconstruction that is probably quite close to the musical reality of Bach's time. It is an irony of reception history that this reconstruction has seen more performances all over the world than Bach's original ever did.

Liturgical Contexts

I have explained in an earlier chapter that Bach's major vocal works were pieces for the liturgy. They were shaped by particular liturgical requirements and they interacted with other elements in the worship services of Bach's time. While today Bach's passions are performed in the concert hall (or as a concert in a church), the pieces were originally liturgical compositions and an integral part of the worship service. I have already outlined the order of the vespers service in Leipzig in Chapter Two. The order on Good Friday afternoon was similar, with a few notable differences:[10]

Hymn: *Da Jesus an dem Kreuze stund*
Passion (part 1)
Hymn: *Herr Jesu Christ, dich zu uns wend*
Sermon (on Bugenhagen's *Passion Harmony*)
Passion (part 2)
Motet: *Ecce, quomodo moritur justus* (Jacob Handl)
Collect prayer
Biblical verse: "Die Strafe liegt auf ihm" (Isaiah 53:5)
Hymn: *Nun danket alle Gott*

The liturgical context of the piece is important because it already gave the listener in 1724 a key for understanding the suffering and death of Jesus. When we listen to the *St John Passion* today we patiently wait in silence before the conductor lifts his baton and the first notes of the opening chorus are played by the orchestra. In Bach's time, the service started with the congregational hymn "Da Jesus an dem Kreuze stund" (When Jesus stood at the cross), a hymn based on Jesus' seven last words at the cross. The chorale is almost a summary of the passion narrative, leading from his crucifixion to his agony and his final cry of divine abandonment.

After this opening hymn follows the first half of Bach's passion, ranging from the opening chorus to movement 14,

"Petrus, der nicht denkt zurück." In a performance in the twenty-first century, we often have a short intermission. The audience can stand up, maybe talk to their neighbor, stretch their legs for a few minutes. In 1724, the congregation stayed put, instead singing a hymn by themselves: "Herr Jesu Christ, dich zu uns wend." It is not a passion hymn but a hymn that asks for God's presence in his word: "Lord Jesus Christ, turn yourself towards us and give us your Holy Spirit that we understand your word." It was commonly sung before the sermon, which would now follow in the order of the liturgy. It is a hymn of preparation for the sermon, but it also looks back to the first half of the passion performance, asking for understanding of the biblical narrative of Christ's suffering.

The sermon was commonly based on a section from Bugenhagen's *Passion Harmony*, the compilation of gospel texts that was also used by Wiegner for his book of passion meditations from 1724. The sermon is already the third interpretation of the passion in the vespers service: first in the opening hymn, then in the first half of Bach's *St John Passion*, and then in the sermon. The actual sermons that were preached with Bach's passions have not come down to us. However, we can already see from the setup in the liturgy that the congregation in the 1720s experienced a multifaceted interpretation of the events of the passion; not much different again from Wiegner's book, which provided the biblical texts, extensive contemplative texts, hymns, and pictorial representations of the events.

After the sermon followed, in the order of the liturgy, the second part of Bach's composition, moving from Jesus' interrogation by Pilate to his scourging, crucifixion, death, and eventually his burial. Immediately following the performance of the passion the choir sang the late sixteenth-century motet

"Ecce, quomodo moritur justus" (Behold how the righteous dies) by the composer Jacob Handl (1550–1591). There was no applause for Bach; not even silence to contemplate the final chords of his work—but instead a piece by another, much older composer, which directed the ear of the listener back to the order of the liturgy. Again, the piece affects the perception of the passion setting by Bach. The entire narrative of the passion is now summarized by an ancient motet:

> Behold how the righteous dies and no one takes notice.
> The righteous are taken away and no one pays attention.
> The righteous has been taken away from present iniquities
> And his memory shall be in peace.
> His place is in peace and he dwells in Zion.
> And his memory shall be in peace.[11]

The vespers service on Good Friday 1724 ended with a prayer, a short scripture reading from the Old Testament, and a hymn of thanksgiving, "Nun danket alle Gott" (Now thank we all our God). Bach's *St John Passion* was an important part of the events of the afternoon but it was not the only thing that happened. The congregation sang hymns, heard a sermon, and contemplated the death of Christ from different angles. The vespers service in and of itself was already a polyphonic interpretation of the passion narrative. We will see that this polyphony also shapes the perspectives within the passion setting by Bach.

John's Theology of Glory

Each one of the four gospels has its own theology and also the theological significance of the suffering and death of Jesus is

interpreted differently by each evangelist. The Gospel according
to Matthew, for instance, emphasizes the suffering of Jesus the
human as a basis for salvation, whereas the Gospel according
to John views the death of Jesus as a demonstration of his
divine glory. This particular Theology of Glory in the Gospel
according to John is already apparent in the opening movement of Bach's *St John Passion*. The first two lines are a direct
quotation from Psalm 8:1 while the following lines were added
by Bach's unknown librettist:

1. Chorus

Herr, unser Herrscher, dessen Ruhm	Lord, our ruler, whose praise
In allen Landen herrlich ist!	Is glorious in all lands!
Zeig uns durch deine Passion,	Show us through your passion
Dass du, der wahre Gottessohn,	That you, the true Son of God,
Zu aller Zeit,	At all times,
Auch in der größten Niedrigkeit,	Even in the greatest humiliation,
Verherrlicht worden bist!	Have been glorified!

Bach's setting underscores this notion of glory: the orchestral
prelude begins with a vivid, circular motive in the strings. The
same musical motive will be combined with the word
"Herrscher" (ruler), a few moments later (example 4.1). The
circular motive and the pulsating bass create energy and project
the feeling of excitement. The choir enters in measure 19 with
massive chords. The voices exclaim three times "Herr" (Lord)
(example 4.2) before the music moves on to praise him as the
glorious ruler of all the lands.

The glory of God is present from measure 1 of the
opening movement. But this glory is, in a truly Johannean
sense, directly linked to Jesus' suffering. While the strings play
their "glory" motive, the oboes and flutes tint the glorious
picture in darker colors, partly overshadowing the sound of

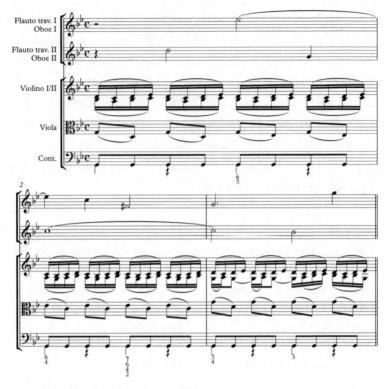

Example 4.1: Bach, *St John Passion* BWV 245/1, mm. 1–3

glory. The wind instruments play dissonant suspensions that contrast with the pure harmonies of the violins and violas (example 4.1). In a later movement (no. 21d), Bach uses similar suspensions when he sets the word "crucify".

In the Gospel according to John, Christ's suffering and glorification are intrinsically intertwined. One is not thinkable without the other. The opening movement of the *St John Passion* makes this clear by layering the motive for God's glory onto that of Christ's suffering and crucifixion. Bach returns to this idea immediately before the death of Jesus. In an alto aria, the singer intones a mournful lament with the text "Es ist

Example 4.2: Bach, *St John Passion* BWV 245/1, mm. 19–22

vollbracht! O Trost vor die gekränkten Seelen! Die Trauernacht
läßt nun die letzte Stunde zählen." (It is accomplished! O
comfort for the afflicted souls! The night of mourning now
counts the final hour.) It is the saddest moment of the passion.
The alto has a dark, descending motive, the music is "molt'
adagio" (very slow) and the viola da gamba—which is only
used as solo instrument in this one movement of the *St John
Passion*—produces a somber sound, drenched with sighing
and mourning. This sad moment is suddenly interrupted by a
celebratory exclamation of the text "Der Held aus Juda siegt
mit Macht und schließt den Kampf" (The hero from Judah
triumphs with power and brings the battle to a close). Bach
abruptly switches the mood: the slow tempo changes to
"vivace" (lively), dark B minor is replaced with brightest D
major, and the viola da gamba is drowned out by fast and vivid
motives in the violins. Most prominent, however, are the
fanfare-like motives sung by the alto. Reminding one of
martial trumpet fanfares, these are the fanfares of victory
(example 4.3). The music eventually reverts to the mourning
tone, but the fanfares preemptively shine the victorious light
of Easter Sunday on the moment of Christ's death.

In the final chorale of the *St John Passion*, Bach returns to
the Theology of Glory. The movement broadens the view to
the return of Christ and the resurrection of the dead at the end
of time. Christ is called the Savior and the "throne of mercy"
and the chorus finally promises:

Herr Jesu Christ, erhöre mich,	Lord Jesus Christ, grant me this;
Ich will dich preisen ewiglich!	I want to praise you eternally!

We are back at the beginning of the passion: the glorification
of Christ in his suffering.

Example 4.3: Bach, *St John Passion* BWV 245/30, mm. 19–22

Text Compilation

I have mentioned the polyphony of voices and views of the passion in the Good Friday vespers in Leipzig in the 1720s. The same applies to the different voices within the *St John Passion*. The libretto for the passion is a mixture of different text genres. The biblical narrative from the Gospel according to John serves as the backbone. The passion story from John 18–19 is presented completely. Most of the text is sung by the tenor; if a larger group is speaking, Bach sets the words as a turba chorus (crowd chorus) for the larger vocal ensemble. If individual characters speak in the narrative, such as Jesus, Peter, and Pilate, these words are sung by other soloists.

The biblical text is frequently interrupted by contemplative interpolations in the form of arias, recitatives, and chorales. This brings us back to the image from Wiegner's book. The free poetry, particularly the meditative arias for soloists, represent the perspective of the individual believer. In her meditations on the passion narrative she becomes a bystander and witness of the events and comments on them from her own viewpoint. The same is true for the hymn stanzas, with the difference that they represent the communal view of the Christian church (or congregation) as a whole.

The free poetic texts for the arias and recitatives were compiled from different sources. Several of the texts for the arias were taken from a passion libretto by Barthold Heinrich Brockes (1680–1747), one of the most successful passion texts in the eighteenth century.[12] The entire Brockes libretto had been set to music by composers such as George Frideric Handel and Georg Philipp Telemann (1681–1767). Bach, on the other hand, only borrowed texts for individual movements. The text by Brockes is known (and notorious) for its very graphic descriptions of the wounds and suffering of Jesus. It transfers the rich colors of baroque passion paintings into poetry. Two of the texts from Brockes are the recitative "Betrachte" and the subsequent aria "Erwäge:"

19. Arioso (Bass)

Betrachte, meine Seel, mit ängstlichem Vergnügen,	Ponder, my soul, with anxious pleasure,
Mit bittrer Lust und halb beklemmtem Herzen	With bitter delight and half-uneasy heart,
Dein höchstes Gut in Jesu Schmerzen,	In Jesus' agonies your highest good;

Wie dir auf Dornen, so ihn stechen,	How, for you, out of the thorns that pierce him,
Die Himmelsschlüsselblumen blühn!	The Key-of-Heaven-flowers blossom!
Du kannst viel süße Frucht von seiner Wermut brechen	You can break off much sweet fruit from his wormwood,
Drum sieh ohn Unterlass auf ihn!	So look on him without ceasing!

20. Aria (Tenor)

Erwäge, wie sein blutgefärbter Rücken	Consider how his blood-tinged back
In allen Stücken	In all aspects
Dem Himmel gleiche geht,	Is just like the sky,
Daran, nachdem die Wasserwogen	Where, after the floodwaves
Von unsrer Sündflut sich verzogen,	Of our sins' deluge have passed by,
Der allerschönste Regenbogen	The most exceedingly beautiful rainbow
Als Gottes Gnadenzeichen steht!	Stands as a sign of God's grace!

The thorns become flowers, and the colors of the wounds on Jesus' back remind the beholder of the rainbow that symbolized the covenant between God and man after Noah's flood. The images might be unfamiliar to us, maybe even repulsive. But we have to remember that they are a way for the beholder to become part of the story—just like James of Milan who had entered the wounds of Jesus in his thirteenth-century meditations.

Other texts in the libretto for the *St John Passion* were taken from writings by Christian Weise (1642–1708) and Christian Heinrich Postel (1658–1705), two poets from the second half of the seventeenth century. For several of the arias we do not know the author. They might have been written by the person who compiled all the texts for the libretto, or they could equally have been selected from other passion texts that have not survived. It is likely that a local poet or theologian in Bach's

Leipzig put all the texts together and probably added some more from his own pen. He also picked the stanzas from congregational hymns that interrupt the libretto at several moments. Finally, the libretto for the *St John Passion* contains several short sections from the Gospel according to Matthew, which are interpolated between the texts from the Gospel according to John. One of these sections is the report about the earthquake after the death of Jesus, which is missing in John but provided the composer with an opportunity to compose particularly dramatic music. We will return to that movement later.

In its polyphony of voices, the *St John Passion* differs significantly from Bach's *St Matthew Passion*. The libretto for the later work was written by one single poet, Christian Friedrich Henrici (1700–1764), who started his collaboration with Bach in 1725. However, even though the texts for the earlier passion were selected from several sources, they were not combined randomly but the compiler arranged them with a clear concept.

The different texts represent different layers of time and space. The biblical text provides the narrative, historically situated in the time of Jesus. The arias (and some of the recitatives) represent the believer, observing and reflecting on the passion of Christ. It is the individual in Bach's time, yet she becomes simultaneously situated in the narrative by immersing herself into the story. The hymns, finally, represent the reaction of the Christian congregation. A few examples will make this pattern clear. During the arrest in the garden of Gethsemane, Jesus says to his arresters:

2e. Jesus

Ich hab's euch gesagt, dass ich's sei, suchet ihr denn mich, so lasset diese gehen!	I have told you I'm that one; if you are looking for me, then let these others go!

The 'imagined congregation' in the following hymn, represented by the choir, replies:

3. Chorale

O große Lieb, o Lieb ohn alle Maße,	O great love, o love beyond all measure,
Die dich gebracht auf diese Marterstraße!	That has brought you on this path of torment!
Ich lebte mit der Welt in Lust und Freuden,	I lived with the world in delight and joy,
Und du musst leiden.	And you have to suffer.

The keyword connection between the hymn and the previous biblical text is the phrase "let these go." In the biblical narrative, the phrase refers to the disciples, whom Jesus asks the soldiers to release. But now in the context of Bach's passion, the imagined congregation asks, "What does that mean for us?" The "pro me" (for me) is one of the core questions of Lutheran hermeneutics. The biblical narrative has to be realized and contextualized for one's own existence. Consequently, the sentence spoken by Jesus, "let these go," has to have a meaning beyond its historical context. And the answer given by the libretto for the *St John Passion* is clear: in the same way Jesus asked the soldiers to let the disciples go, the faithful believers can go because Jesus suffered and died for their sins.

A similar example, now with the reflection of the individual, appears a few movements later. The evangelist reports:

8. Evangelist

Simon Petrus aber folgete Jesu nach und ein ander Jünger.	Simon Peter, however, and another disciple followed Jesus.

Again, the historical event of Peter following Jesus has to be recontextualized by the believer observing the scene. Just as Peter set out to follow Jesus, the believer promises Jesus to follow him.

9. Aria (Soprano)

Ich folge dir gleichfalls mit freudigen Schritten	I will follow you likewise with joyful steps
Und lasse dich nicht,	And will not let you [go],
Mein Leben, mein Licht.	My life, my light.
Befördre den Lauf	Pave the way
Und höre nicht auf,	And do not stop
Selbst an mir zu ziehen, zu schieben, zu bitten.	Drawing, shoving, imploring me yourself.

It is interesting to observe how Bach transfers this text into music. Several of the words in the libretto were predestined to guide the imagination of a baroque composer: the following, the joyful steps, and the drawing and shoving lend themselves to an expressive musical setting. The idea of following was easy to express in music: the two voices follow one another. One begins with a musical motive; then the second one enters a short time later (example 4.4). The word "joyful" is likewise expressed in the joyful 16th-note motion.

Example 4.4: Bach, *St John Passion* BWV 245/9, mm. 17–20

The words "drawing" and "shoving," in the second half of the aria text, were a bigger challenge for the composer. Drawing and shoving requires a lot of effort; it leads to hesitation in the movement; interrupts the flow of motion. The movement becomes a little tenacious. Bach transfers this idea into music by means of chromatic half-tone steps. We can hear the effort Christ puts into drawing and shoving the believer in the right direction.

Another important detail about this aria, both in the music and the text, is the significant Lutheran theological tenet regarding what humans do and what God does. Salvation, for Luther and theologians in the Lutheran tradition, is always the consequence of divine agency. The human contribution can only be a reaction to the divine action. In the words of the aria, the believer cannot follow Jesus through her own power, not without Jesus' drawing and shoving. This is, in the colorful language of baroque poetry, the dichotomy between works and faith. The duality between divine agency and human reaction is also reflected in the music. The joyful promise to follow Jesus is set in clear, diatonic motives at the beginning of the aria, while the divine contribution is fashioned as a sharp contrast in chromatic motives.

Changing Contexts – Changing Functions

When Bach and his collaborator on the libretto borrowed text from other libretti, the text sometimes acquired a new function within its new context. This close connection between texts and contexts becomes particularly clear in the case of the movement "Von den Stricken," borrowed from Brockes's passion oratorio:

7. Aria (Alto)

Von den Stricken meiner Sünden	To unbind me
Mich zu entbinden,	From the ropes of my sins,
Wird mein Heil gebunden.	My Salvation is bound.
Mich von allen Lasterbeulen	To heal me fully
Völlig zu heilen,	From all my vice-boils,
Läßt er sich verwunden.	He lets himself be wounded.

In Brockes's passion, the text serves as the opening movement for the passion. We have seen in the first movement of Bach's *St John Passion* how his opening chorus sets the tone for the entire piece, highlighting the glory of God as the precondition for salvation. In a similar way, the opening movement in Brockes's text sets the stage for the following piece: the suffering of Christ as basis for salvation. The binding of Christ leads to release of the bondage of sin; the wounds of Christ heal the inflictions of these sins. The spotlight in Brockes's libretto is not on God's Glory, but on the physical reality of Jesus' suffering and death. It is closer to the human Jesus in the Gospel according to Matthew than the divine Christ in John. The text from Brockes would have been out of place as an opening movement for Bach's *St John Passion*; however, it could be used as an interpolation during the narrative. The gospel text reports the binding of Jesus and the decision of Caiaphas, that it would be good if someone was killed to appease the people:

6. Evangelist

Die Schar aber und der Oberhauptmann und die Diener der Jüden nahmen Jesum und bunden ihn und führeten ihn	The band, however, and the captain and the attendants of the Jews took Jesus and bound him and led him at first to

aufs erste zu Hannas, der war Kaiphas Schwäher, welcher des Jahres Hoherpriester war. Es war aber Kaiphas, der den Jüden riet, es wäre gut, dass ein Mensch würde umbracht für das Volk.	Annas, the father-in-law of Caiaphas, the one who was high priest in that year. But it was Caiaphas who advised the Jews it would be good that one man be put to death for the people.

This is the moment when Bach and his unknown collaborator insert the Brockes text. The "ropes of sins" now repersent the ropes that are used to bind Jesus; and the phrase "for the people" is reinterpreted as "for me" as in "to unbind me."[13] While the movement was not appropriate as a "headline" for the entire piece, it fit perfectly as a theological interpretation of this particular moment in the passion narrative.

Layers of Meaning

The hymns in Bach's passions and oratorios stand for the reflection on the passion by the whole congregation, while the arias represent the reflections by the individual. In a few instances, Bach combines these two layers of reflection into one movement. He does what language alone could not comprehensively do—combine two texts at the same time. In the penultimate aria of the passion, the two layers, congregational response and individual reflection, converge. Bach juxtaposes the protestant hymn "Jesu, der du warest tot" (Jesus, you who were dead) with the free poetic text "Mein teurer Heiland, laß dich fragen" (My precious Savior, let me ask you). The two layers are interwoven in an intricate dialogue (the chorale is printed here in bold):

32. *Aria (Bass) and choir*

Mein teurer Heiland, laß dich fragen,	My precious Savior, let me ask you:
Jesu, der du warest tot,	**Jesus, you who were dead,**
Da du nunmehr ans Kreuz geschlagen	Since you were nailed to the cross
Und selbst gesagt: Es ist vollbracht,	And have yourself said, "It is accomplished,"
Lebest nun ohn Ende,	**[But] now lives without end;**
Bin ich vom Sterben frei gemacht?	Have I been made free from death?
In der letzten Todesnot	**In the final throes of death,**
Nirgend mich hinwende	**[I] turn myself nowhere**
Kann ich durch deine Pein und Sterben	Can I through your pain and death
Das Himmelreich ererben?	Inherit the Kingdom of Heaven?
Ist aller Welt Erlösung da?	Is redemption of all the world here?
Als zu dir, der mich versühnt,	**But to you, who reconciled me [with God],**
O du lieber Herre!	**O you dear Lord!**
Du kannst vor Schmerzen zwar nichts sagen;	You can, in agony, it is true, say nothing;
Gib mir nur, was du verdient,	**Give me only what you have merited;**
Doch neigest du das Haupt	But you bow your head
Und sprichst stillschweigend: ja.	And say in silence, "Yes."
Mehr ich nicht begehre!	**More I do not desire!**

The text of the aria asks what the death of Jesus meant for the individual: "Bin ich vom Sterben frei gemacht? [. . .] Kann ich durch deine Pein und Sterben das Himmelreich ererben?" (Have I been made free from death? . . . Can I through your pain and death inherit the Kingdom of Heaven?). The hymn, the voice of the church, gives the answer: "Jesu, der du warest tot, lebest nun ohn Ende." The hymn (the church) already understands salvation through resurrection while the individual has doubts.[14] Only at the end is the believer convinced by the hope that is promised by the hymn, "Du kannst vor Schmerzen zwar nichts sagen; doch neigest du das Haupt und sprichst stillschweigend: ja." (You can, in agony, it is true, say nothing; but you bow your head and say in silence, "Yes.") The turning point in this dialogue is the moment when the chorale layer calls Jesus "Lord." The bass drops out for a moment. It is the first time that the soloist and the chorale do not sound at the same time. It is the very moment when Jesus is—in a truly Johannean sense—addressed as the Lord ("Herr"). The moment the hymn identifies Jesus as ruler (and thus death and crucifixion as a demonstration of his glory), the individual believer is ready to confess that the death of Jesus is the manifestation of his power. Similarly, the dropping of Jesus' head at the moment of his death is not the end but rather him nodding "yes" to the believer.

In this example, Bach employs contrast to interpret and emphasize the text. In the following sequence of movements, Bach uses musical unity to explore the meaning(s) of the biblical narrative. It is the scene immediately after the death of Jesus. The biblical text reports the tearing of the veil in the temple and describes the subsequent earthquake:

33. Evangelist

Und siehe da, der Vorhang im Tempel zerriß in zwei Stück von oben an bis unten aus. Und die Erde erbebete, und die Felsen zerrissen, und die Gräber täten sich auf, und stunden auf viel Leiber der Heiligen.

And look: the veil in the Temple was rent in two pieces, from top to bottom. And the earth quaked, and the rocks rent, and the graves opened, and the bodies of many saints arose.

The earthquake scene of course is not from the Gospel according to John but from Matthew 27:51–2. The short text was inserted for two reasons. Firstly, all four gospels were for a Christian in the early eighteenth century the Word of God even though details might differ. The *Passion Harmony* by Bugenhagen even provided an amalgamation of the four passion narratives. Inserting a section from one gospel into the narrative of another did not pose a problem in a time before historical-critical exegesis; instead, it provided a more complete and robust picture. And secondly, the earthquake was a detail of the passion narrative a librettist and a composer did not want to miss in a dramatic passion setting. The shaking of the earth provided an opportunity for an effective musical composition, as well as for a theological interpretation that employed the natural catastrophe to move the affects and emotions of the listener. In the first version of Bach's *St John Passion* from 1724, the librettist inserted the passage from Mark, which has the tearing of the veil but not the earthquake. Only in the second version from 1725 did Bach (and his librettist) employ the even more dramatic passage from the Gospel according to Matthew. In the version from 1732, Bach eliminated the text from Matthew again but finally brought it back in the last version from the late 1740s.[15]

Some of our earlier examples have shown how the libretto takes phrases and ideas from the biblical narrative and interprets them in an updated, personal fashion. The same happens with musical ideas. Bach clearly knows how to exploit the dramatic possibilities the text has to offer (example 4.5). We see the tearing of the veil in the basso continuo line in measure 3. A rapid line of 32nd notes races down over two octaves from e' to low D. In the following measure, depicting the text "die Erde erbebete" (the earth quaked), Bach sets trembling

Example 4.5: Bach, *St John Passion* BWV 245/33, mm. 1–7

bass notes in a low register; listeners hear and even feel the trembling underneath the declamation of the text by the tenor.

The hermeneutic question that a preacher in Bach's time would now ask is, "what does that mean?" The following accompanied arioso for tenor provides a part of the answer:

34. Arioso (Tenor)

Mein Herz, in dem die ganze Welt	My heart—while the entire world
Bei Jesu Leiden gleichfalls leidet,	With Jesus' suffering likewise suffers,
Die Sonne sich in Trauer kleidet,	The sun clothes itself in mourning,
Der Vorhang reißt, der Fels zerfällt,	The veil tears, the rock crumbles,

Die Erde bebt, die Gräber spalten,	The earth quakes, the graves split open,
Weil sie den Schöpfer sehn erkalten,	Because they see the creator growing cold—
Was willst du deines Ortes tun?	What will you do for your part?

While the text recounts some of the events in nature—the clothing of the sun, the tearing of the veil, the quaking of the earth—it draws attention to the human heart and asks, "what will you do for your part?" Bach's setting features the musical motives we would expect (example 4.6): a descending line in

Example 4.6: Bach, *St John Passion* BWV 245/34, mm. 5–6

measure 5, when the text mentions the tearing of the veil; rapidly repeated notes when we learn about the trembling of the earth (measure 6). However, the beginning of the arioso is most intriguing. Even before the text mentions the trembling of the earth, Bach inserts the trembling figure in measures 1 and 3. It is the same motive he will use to depict the earthquake in measure 5, but here it is the trembling (or rather beating) of the heart of the believer who observes the death of Christ and the subsequent earthquake. In the engraving in Wiegner's book it is the heart where the encounter between Christ and the believer takes place. The believer's heart burns with desire for Christ. Consequently here, the heart of the believer starts to beat faster in the face of the events surrounding Christ's death.

The arioso serves as a bridge between the narrative and the following aria. The soprano aria goes one step further in interpreting the biblical events:

35. Aria (Soprano)

Zerfließe, mein Herze, in Fluten der Zähren	Dissolve, my heart, in floods of tears
Dem Höchsten zu Ehren!	To honor the Most High!
Erzähle der Welt und dem Himmel die Not:	Declare to the world and to Heaven the distress:
Dein Jesus ist tot!	Your Jesus is dead!

The focus is again on the heart as the place of human-divine encounter: "Dissolve, my heart, in floods of tears." But now the earthquake is not mentioned at all. The spotlight is on the human response to the events. The events themselves, with the exception of the death of Jesus, have disappeared. Only the music still preserves the memory of the trembling that had shaken both the earth and the human heart (example 4.7).

Example 4.7: Bach, *St John Passion* BWV 245/35, mm. 1–10

The repeated notes in the instrumental bass (measures 1–6), as well as the repetitions in the flute and oboe da caccia (measures 9–11), remind us of the repetitive trembling in the gospel recitative and the arioso. It is a fascinating example of Bach transforming a musical motive to reveal a deeper meaning. The trembling motion ties together the three movements that theologically belong together, the gospel recitative, the tenor arioso, and the soprano aria. The hermeneutic background for this is again the Lutheran view of biblical interpretation, asking for the *pro me* (for me). What do the historical events mean for the believer here and now? The transformation of the musical motives explores this question, departing from the biblical narrative and then showing its metaphorical value: the earthquake of our hearts.

The image of the "earthquake of the heart" was a familiar one in the German Lutheran sermon tradition of Bach's time. The seventeenth-century preacher Heinrich Müller (1631–1675) in his *Evangelische Schluß-kett* (a book owned by Bach) draws a similar connection between the earthquake and the anxious beating of the believer's heart:

Die Erde bebete für Christo, ja für ihn beben alle irdischen HErtzen. Denn die ihm angehören, müssen der Welt gecreutziget seyn, creutzigen ihr Fleisch samt den Lüsten und Begierden, und ihm sein Creutz nachtragen ... Das HErtz bebet ihnen für Angst, wann sie mercken, daß sie von einem Fehl übereilet, ja, wann sie auch nur, gleich wider ihren Willen, eine böse Lust empfinden. Sie dienen dem HErrn mit furcht, und freuen sich mit Zittern.[16]

The earth quaked for Christ, yes, for him quake all hearts on earth. Because those who belong to him, have to be crucified to be separated from the world, they crucify their flesh and their lust and desires, and carry the cross for him ... Their hearts tremble in fear when they notice that they have failed, even if they feel an evil desire against their own will. They serve the Lord with fear and rejoice with trembling.

We will return to Müller's sermons and their influence on the theology of Bach's major works when we explore the smaller oratorios for Easter Sunday and Ascension Day in Chapter Six.

For Me – But Who Am I?

The hermeneutic principle of the "for me," which in the case of the earthquake leads to a very personal interpretation of this natural phenomenon, inevitably begs the question, "who is this 'me'? Who am I?" It is the question of identity. And indeed, the words "ich" and "mich"—I and me—are of particular significance in Bach's *St John Passion*. They are connected to concepts of identity in general: who is Jesus and who are his disciples? Who is, and what constitutes, the faithful believer?

   Let us return to the opening scene of the passion. When
the soldiers search the garden of Gethsemane and inquire
about "Jesus of Nazareth," he answers, "Ich bin's" (That I am).
Bach sets the words with a strong cadence, reflecting the
power and confidence of the divine response (example 4.8a).
A similar question is posed a few moments later, albeit with
a different outcome. We see Peter outside the high priest's
house. He is sitting at a fire, warming himself. A maid
asks him, "Aren't you one of this man's disciples?" The honest
response would have been the same as the one given by
Jesus in the garden, "Ich bin's" (That I am), sung with a similarly assertive cadence. However, Peter denies any association
with "that man" and sings, "Ich bin's nicht" (That I am not).
Bach's setting immediately reveals the deception (example
4.8b). The composer begins on the same note (d) and also

Example 4.8: Bach, *St John Passion* BWV 245/2 a) mm. 22–3; b) mm. 14–15

ends on the same note (g). However, Peter's response takes a detour, leaping higher first and then climbing down two steps. Peter is shifty and so is the music. Even more revealing is the instrumental accompaniment. The word "I" is challenged by a dissonant chord and the following measure lacks a bass note on the first beat altogether. An attentive listener will immediately notice that something is wrong. This is not the assertive cadence of Jesus' answer; this is not the truth. Peter is lying.

Jesus replies "That I am;" Peter says "That I am not." The text for the passion poses a third question, now in a hymn stanza: "Wer hat dich so geschlagen?" (Who has struck you so?). The answer is given by the second stanza of the hymn, which follows immediately: "Ich, ich und meine Sünden" (I, I, and my sins). The congregation joins Jesus and Peter in their quest for identity. Jesus reveals himself confidently; Peter denies his identity as Jesus' disciple. And the church, the community of saints, confesses to be a community of sinners: I am the reason for Christ's suffering. In other words, it is "for me" (or for us) that Christ had to suffer and die. Again, the quest for identity is answered by the Lutheran pro me, for me.

"I", "my", and "me" are probably some of the most frequent words in the libretto for the *St John Passion*, especially in the reflective arias. Here are just a few:

- To unbind *me* from the ropes of *my* sins (no. 7)
- *I* will follow you (no. 9)
- *My* precious Savior (no. 32)
- Dissolve, *my* heart (no. 35)

We are again reminded of the first image in Wiegner's book, the believer observing the passion of Christ, interpreting the events from her own perspective, contemplating the death of Christ in her burning heart.

Christ's Death and Our Death

The individualization of the events culminates in the final movements of the *St John Passion*. Luther and his successors had rejected the medieval idea of Purgatory.[17] Instead, death was understood as sleep. The dead did not suffer and repent for their sins in a place of punishment and purification, but rather were suspended in a sleep-like state, waiting for the end of time. This view explains why the penultimate movement of the *St John Passion* has the character of a lullaby. It is a piece in a lilting $\frac{3}{4}$ meter, featuring quiet descending melodic lines in the voice parts. The text wishes the bones of Christ's dead body rest and piece. The believer promises to stop shedding tears herself and instead to contemplate her own death, which is now redeemed through the death of Christ. The redemptory death has finally opened the doors of Heaven and at the same time locked hell once and for all:

39. Chorus

Ruht wohl, ihr heiligen Gebeine,	Be fully at peace, you holy bones,
Die ich nun weiter nicht beweine,	Which I will no longer bewail;
Ruht wohl und bringt auch mich zur Ruh!	Be fully at peace and bring also me to his peace!
Das Grab, so euch bestimmet ist	The grave–which is appointed to you
Und ferner keine Not umschließt,	And from now on no distress will enclose–
Macht mir den Himmel auf und schließt die Hölle zu.	Opens Heaven to me and closes hell.

The final movement, a four-part chorale setting, immediately builds a bridge to the death of the believer:

40. Chorale

Ach Herr, laß dein' lieb' Engelein	Oh Lord, let your dear angels
Am letzten End' die Seele mein	At the very end carry my soul
In Abrahams Schoß tragen;	To Abraham's bosom,
Den Leib in sein'm Schlafkämmerlein	And let my body rest in its little sleeping chamber
Gar sanft, ohn' ein'ge Qual und Pein,	Completely in peace, without any sorrow and pain,
Ruhn bis am Jüngsten Tage!	Until the Last Day!

The chorale setting combines the Lutheran understanding of death as sleep with the highly individual perspective of the passion of Christ in Johann Sebastian Bach's *St John Passion*. The burial of Jesus turns into a meditation of one's own burial. And the hope for Christ's resurrection after three days is the foundation for the resurrection of the dead at the end of time.

The believer in Wiegner's image is not only a bystander, but a participant. She is removed from the historical events by time and space, but she carries Christ in her burning heart. She participates in his death and resurrection. And in good Johannean fashion, she also participates in the glorification of God, as the final lines of the chorale state:

Alsdann vom Tod erwecke mich,	Then raise me from the dead,
Daß meine Augen sehen dich	So that my eyes will look on you
In aller Freud', o Gottes Sohn,	In all joy, o Son of God,
Mein Heiland und Genadenthron!	My Savior and Throne of Grace!
Herr Jesu Christ, erhöre mich,	Lord Jesus Christ, grant me this;
Ich will dich preisen ewiglich!	I want to praise you eternally!

All folds into one. The individual believer is also part of the larger Communion of Saints, the church. The final hymn expresses the confidence of the Church and the hope of the individual. The suffering and death of Christ are simultaneously a manifestation of his glory and thus give reason to look forward to the end of time and to praise Jesus Christ eternally. And the final lines again make statements about the individual: "raise *me* from the dead; *my* eyes; *my* Savior; *I* want to praise you." The quest for individual identity has been answered: the individual and her sins are responsible for Jesus' death; but because of his death and his glory that is revealed in this very death, she has the promise of redemption and she becomes the one who witnesses this divine glory with eternal praise.

CHAPTER FIVE

THE PASSION AND THE PASSIONS
THE ST MATTHEW PASSION BWV 244

I will give my heart to you; sink into it! (BWV 244/13)

The English journal *Athenaeum*, one of the leading journals on art, music, and literature of its time, ran a review of a performance of the *St Matthew Passion* in 1877: "Without dwelling on the repeated attempts to popularize the St Matthew Passion music in London at various times, the plain truth is that it has no hold on public opinion, however ardent is the admiration of artists. The prediction that Bach would extinguish or rival Handel has proved quite false. The 'Messiah' stands unimpaired in attraction, and the Passion music, at every revival in secular buildings, is listened to reverently but will not fill the hall in which it is given."[1] And the reviewer later continues: ". . . a strain of sadness pervades the score; so much so, indeed, that it is utterly impossible to perform the seventy eight numbers in their entirety, so depressing is the iteration of grief."[2]

No doubt, George Frideric Handel's *Messiah* better reflected the esthetics of Victorian England. There was also a certain degree of national pride in the preference of the English composer, Handel, over the German, Bach, when the reviewer compared the *St Matthew Passion* and *Messiah*—the German heritage of Handel notwithstanding. But there is something in the review we might agree with: *Messiah* is probably the piece that is more appealing and easier to listen to. And the texts about the passion of Christ in Handel's oratorio are embedded into a larger context, which leads immediately from Good Friday to Easter Sunday. In about three hours, Handel covers the entire salvation history; Bach recounts in the same time less than three days of Christ's life, focusing, as the reviewer laments, on the "depressing ... iteration of grief."

This essay will outline the history and the characteristics of Bach's passion and I will illustrate that the piece is far less depressing than it seems. In fact, Bach and his librettist view the story of Christ's suffering as an intimate love story.

Bach's Passion in the Liturgy

During his tenure at the St Thomas Church in Leipzig, Johann Sebastian Bach had to perform a large-scale setting of the passion of Christ annually on Good Friday afternoon. While he occasionally performed works by other composers— for example a passion by Gotha Kapellmeister Gottfried Heinrich Stölzel (1690–1749) in 1734—most of the works were written by Bach himself. He created settings based on the four evangelists, two of which, the passions according to Mark and Luke, are lost. The *St Mark Passion* can be partly recon- structed while the *St Luke Passion* is irrevocably lost. The two extant passions, based on the Gospels according to John and Matthew, saw numerous performances during Bach's tenure and most of these performances went along with smaller or greater revisions. The previous chapter has shown how the

St John Passion underwent several stages between 1724 and the late 1740s.

Bach's *St Matthew Passion* is arguably one of his most popular and esteemed works. It was composed during Bach's fourth year in Leipzig, and was performed first during the Good Friday vespers on April 11, 1727; a second performance followed two years later in 1729.[3] The version the congregation heard in 1727 and 1729 was somewhat different from what we are accustomed to hearing in modern performances. Bach reworked the piece significantly for Good Friday 1736. In this revision, the composer further elaborated the separation of the ensemble into two distinct choirs and orchestras, creating a work of monumental dimensions.

As I explained at the beginning of the previous chapter, the passions were composed for the liturgy. They are liturgical pieces and they were embedded into the context of both the Good Friday service and the liturgical year at large. The performance of the Passion in April 1727 marked the end of 'musical fasting.' The liturgies in Bach's churches in Leipzig were normally filled with music: cantatas before the sermon, and more music during the distribution of the Lord's Supper. During Lent, however, concerted music (music with voices and instruments) was strictly prohibited. Between March 2 and April 11, 1727, the congregation at St Thomas in Leipzig would only have sung simple hymns, while the instruments had to remain silent. Private celebrations with music and public musical performances were also banned. We can hardly imagine the impact the first measures of the *St Matthew Passion* had on its original listeners: the long instrumental prelude with its flowing rhythm and the musical motive that gradually expands the musical space; a space that had been left almost void during the forty days of sonic fasting that preceded Good Friday.

In addition to this larger context of the liturgical year, the passion also has its clear place and function in the liturgy of Good Friday. The service would have begun at 1:45 P.M. with a hymn, a poetic rendition of the seven last words of Jesus on the cross. Then the first part of the *St Matthew Passion* was performed, narrating the final days of Jesus' life: the decision of the authorities to arrest him, the Lord's Supper, his betrayal by Judas, and the arrest. The congregation would have to wait for the second half of the passion for more than an hour; first, they would sing a hymn and listen to an hour-length sermon. The second part of the passion, narrating the trial and the crucifixion of Jesus, was followed by a Latin motet, prayers, and a final hymn of thanksgiving. The congregation that attended the first performances of the *St Matthew Passion* during Bach's lifetime had the opportunity to reflect on the suffering of Christ in a multitude of ways: by singing Jesus' last words, by listening to Bach's setting, and by paying attention to the sermon.

The *St Matthew Passion* is a sermon in and of itself. Bach not only sets the biblical narrative as a musical drama—with dialogues between soloists and interjections of the 'crowd' in choir settings—but also theologically interprets the biblical text, exploring the meaning of the narrative for the contemporary listener. The previous chapter on Bach's *St John Passion* has demonstrated that the interpretation of the biblical text in arias and recitatives follows the hermeneutic principle of asking, "What does it mean for me?" – "Why and how are the historical events relevant for the contemporary listener?" The image from Wiegner's passion meditations was a visual representation of this principle. The believer became a beholder of the events and her heart was stirred by what she observed. The text of the *St Matthew Passion* follows the same concept. This becomes clear in one of the early scenes of the work: Jesus celebrates Passover with his disciples and announces to them that one of the twelve will betray him. The evangelist reports: "And they became very distressed, and started, each and every one among them, to say to him: Lord, am I the one?" (nos. 9d and e). The following movement includes the contemporary believers in this conversation by inserting a hymn stanza, commonly the voice of the congregation (as the community of believers):

10. Chorale

Ich bin's, ich sollte büßen,	I am the one, I should atone:
An Händen und an Füßen	Bound, hand and foot,
Gebunden in der Höll.	In hell.
Die Geißeln und die Banden	The scourges and the bonds
Und was du ausgestanden,	And what you have endured –
Das hat verdienet meine Seel.	My soul has merited that.

While the disciples in the historical narrative are still pondering the question of who might be the betrayer, the Christian congregation confesses its responsibility for the suffering and death of Christ.

Structure

As brilliant as the theological message of this example is, it was not Bach's idea but, rather, the genius of the librettist. The text for the *St Matthew Passion* was not written by the composer himself but by Christian Friedrich Henrici, known by his pen-name Picander (1700–1764)—a local poet who frequently provided Bach with texts for his sacred and secular music. The music of the passion is so strong that we tend to forget that the piece was the product of a collaboration between librettist and composer.

The structure of Bach's *St Matthew Passion* follows an old format that goes back to the Middle Ages, when the text of the passion was chanted, based on simple melodic models. This practice continued past the Lutheran Reformation and well into Bach's time. The chanting of the passion was commonly framed by a short introduction, the so-called *exordium*, and a final movement, the *conclusio*. These framing sections could be simple announcements that this was the story of the suffering and death of Jesus Christ, but they would increasingly become the place for a theological statement, interpreting the meaning of this death. We find a similar framework in the text of Bach's passion. The piece begins with a large-scale choral movement "Kommt, ihr Töchter" and ends with another choral movement at the end, bidding farewell to the body of Christ.

In addition to this interpretative frame, musical settings of the passion over time included increasingly dramatic features and reflective interpolations. The easiest way to make the cantilation of the text more interesting (and dramatic) was to divide the text into dialogue for three or more people and to assign the words spoken by a crowd to a small chorus. This chorus would, in the course of the sixteenth century, sing the words of the crowd in a little polyphonic section, while the rest of the passion was still chanted.

In a further step of interpretation and dramatization, composers of passions in the seventeenth century inserted stanzas from congregational hymns into the passion. The texts of the stanzas would highlight the meaning of certain aspects of the narrative and give the setting a specific focus. Only reluctantly would free poetry become a part of the liturgical passion setting. We first find traces in extra-liturgical pieces, works that were performed for spiritual edification during Lent, before free poetic texts found their way into the liturgical passions in the late seventeenth and early eighteenth centuries. Bach's passions stand at the culmination of this development; however, the conservative liturgical traditions in Leipzig still required him to maintain the unaltered gospel texts from the Luther Bible as the backbone for the passion libretto. At institutions that were more modern than St Thomas in Leipzig, even the biblical text could appear in free poetic paraphrase.[4]

The inclusion of instrumental music in liturgical passions was also somewhat contested. Most liturgical traditions prohibited the use of instruments during Lent, and the majority of passion settings did not use any instruments to accompany the singers until the middle of the seventeenth century. In Leipzig, it was not until the early 1720s that composers were permitted to use instruments in the Good Friday services of the two main churches. Instrumental music was still prohibited during Lent, but an exception was granted for the afternoon service on Good Friday.

The historical overview helps us to understand the structure of the *St Matthew Passion*. The passion grew out of the practice of liturgical cantilation; the biblical text is sung in its entirety, mostly by the tenor (evangelist). Hymn stanzas and interpretative sections that reflect on the theological meaning of the passion narrative are interpolated into this framework. The biblical text is broken up into sections, each one followed by theological interpretation and contemplative reflections. Then follows a new segment of the biblical text, and the pattern repeats. The structure of the piece is determined by the narrative, which then triggers reflective responses.

We can visualize this as three layers. The first layer is the biblical text, the narration of Christ's passion. The second layer consists of the arias and some of the recitatives: these represent the responses of the individual believer. They are often very personal in tone and highly expressive. The third layer is the hymns, representing the voice of the congregation (or the Church in general). We know that the congregation in Leipzig did not sing these hymns during the performance, but they nevertheless perceived them very much as "their songs."

A paradigmatic example of how Bach's *St Matthew Passion* is structured appears quite early in the piece: Jesus and his disciples come into the garden of Gethsemane and Jesus asks them to wait for him while he prays. He also admits that his "soul is distressed to the point of death." The setting of the biblical text begins with the narration of the evangelist (no. 18), set by Bach as a sparsely accompanied ("secco") recitative in declamatory fashion. The words of Jesus, on the other hand, are accompanied by the strings, creating the impression of a halo around his words. Bach uses a similar accompaniment for all the words of Jesus, differentiating them clearly and sonically from the rest of the dialogue. There is only one exception to this practice, and this is encountered much later in the passion when the words "Eli, Eli, lama asabthani" (My God, my God, why have you forsaken me?) are unaccompanied, lacking this musical halo. Jesus feels not only abandoned by God, but his musical halo has also vanished for a moment. In this earlier scene, however, the halo is still present. The strings accompany the voice of Jesus, sung by a bass. The second time the bass enters, we hear not only a sonic halo but also a repeated, beating motive. The text of this section describes Jesus' desperation, and the repeated chords in the strings can easily be heard as a depiction of the beating of his heart (example 5.1).

The following recitative, sung by the tenor (no. 19), reflects on what this means for the believer: "O Schmerz! Hier zittert das gequälte Herz; wie sinkt es hin, wie bleicht sein Angesicht!"

Example 5.1: Bach, *St Matthew Passion* BWV 244/18, mm. 12–15

(O agony! Here the afflicted heart trembles; how it sinks to the ground, how his face pales!). The text of the recitative is a reaction to the pain of Jesus in the garden. We can almost imagine a spectator to this scene watching from afar and reflecting on this suffering. Bach's setting of the text draws a connection between the biblical narrative and the following commentary. The instrumental bass line features a repeated note that continues the "heartbeat" from the previous movement. This bass motive is then combined with a new musical idea in the accompanying instruments, a sigh-like motive, played by the two flutes and two oboes. The sigh-motive reflects the text "O agony," while the following line, "the afflicted heart trembles," is sonically depicted by the pulsating of the bass line (example 5.2).

Example 5.2: Bach, *St Matthew Passion* BWV 244/19, mm. 1–3

Bach now combines these individual reflections on the suffering of Christ with a four-part hymn setting, representing the view of the congregation. The first line of the hymn asks about the meaning of this suffering, "Was ist die Ursach aller solcher Plagen?" (What is the cause of all such torments?), and the following line provides the reply: "Ach! Meine Sünden haben dich geschlagen!" (Ah! My sins have struck you!). The logic of the text is clear: the biblical narrative leads to contemplation by the individual on this suffering, and then to the communal confession of sin. This combination of musical and textual layers represents the model for most of the texts of the *St Matthew Passion*. The individual and the communal responses are not always so intertwined, but we can continue to detect a dialogue between biblical narrative, individual reflection, and communal response.

Love

While the biblical texts had to remain unaltered, the arias and hymns left ample room for interpretation. These interpretations have a strong focus on love on the one hand and on a graphic and dramatic depiction of Christ's suffering on the other. These two contrasting affects seem to be contradictory to a modern listener; and we find numerous accounts in the nineteenth and twentieth centuries of performance cutting some of the hard-to-understand sections and focusing more on the dramatic moments of the setting of the biblical narrative. The love poetry, however, and the emphasis on the cruel suffering of Christ (including an almost voyeuristic focus on his blood and wounds) are not only an important part of the theological profile of the *St Matthew Passion*, but they are actually intrinsically intertwined.

The opening chorus of the *St Matthew Passion* sets the stage for this understanding of the passion. The movement juxtaposes two choirs and two orchestras, one representing the *Daughter of Zion* and the other the *Believers*: "Come, you Daughters, help me lament, look," the *Daughter of Zion* commands, and the *Believers* ask "at whom?" The *Daughter of Zion* replies, "The bridegroom," and we learn later that the *Believers* have to behold him "just like a lamb" because he is about to be killed. All of this

happens "out of love and favor." The opening movement admonishes the listener to hear the passion as something that Christ,
the bridegroom, who loves the bride, the believer, has done out
of love. His suffering and pain stand as a testament to his love.

Bach's setting of Picander's multi-layered text begins
with a majestic instrumental introduction which invokes
eighteenth-century conventions of pastoral, shepherds' music:
a lilting $\frac{12}{8}$ meter, a static bass line, flowing motives in the
upper voices. But Bach immediately destroys this pastoral
impression by introducing harsh dissonances and a texture
that is rhythmically too complex for a shepherds' song. The
allusions to the pastoral sphere are clearly motivated by the
reference to the lamb, but the setting also asserts that we are
leaving the harmonious, bucolic world. The beholder is about
to witness the slaughtering of the sacrificial lamb.

When the voices enter in measure 17, Bach juxtaposes the
two ensembles in blocks, resembling seventeenth-century
polychoral techniques. The two choirs are kept distinct until
the moment when the text explains the motivation for Christ's
suffering, the "love and favor;" now the two ensembles are
joined, highlighting the central idea of the text. Bach divides
them again only when he returns to the text from the beginning. We will see later how the movement serves as a "headline" for the whole passion setting.

The opening chorus of the *St Matthew Passion* welcomes
Christ as the bridegroom. The bride/bridegroom imagery,
derived from the *Song of Songs*, describes the concept of *unio
mystica*, mystic unity between the believer and Christ. Around
1700, the theological term that described this unity in Lutheran
theology was *inhabitatio* (indwelling), which denotes the
dwelling of Christ in the human heart. We have explored this
concept in Chapter Three as the underlying idea of the *Christmas*

Oratorio. Johann Arndt (1555–1621), one of the most influential religious authors from the first half of the seventeenth
century, whose four *Books on True Christianity* shaped Protestant
piety like no other in the baroque period, describes the unity
between Christ and the believer in his 1620 treatise *De unione
credentium cum Christo capite ecclesiae* (The unity of the believers
with Christ, the head of the church). The German translation
(published later that same year) was subsequently incorporated
in the extended version of Arndt's popular book on Christianity,
the *Six Books on True Christianity*, thus becoming part of a widely
read book of religious edification. For Arndt, the goal of human
life is the unification with God;[5] the communion between God
and the believer is established through God's word (as God is
present in his word) and through the sacraments:

Im Wort aber und H. Sacramenten ist das rechte Gedächtniß des Namens GOttes gestiftet. Darum wird er auch durch das Wort und Sacrament mit uns vereiniget. Welches unser Heyland mit dem schönen und lieblichen Spruch bekräftiget: Wer mich liebet, der wird mein Wort halten, und mein Vatter wird ihn lieben, und wir werden zu ihm kommen und Wohnung bey ihm machen (Joh. 14,13).[6]	In the word and in the holy sacraments is laid down the true memory of the name of God. That is why he is unified with us through the word and the sacrament; which was confirmed by the Savior through the beautiful and lovely saying: He who loves me will keep my word and my father will love him and we will come to him and dwell with him (John 14:13).

In other words, *inhabitatio*—the mystical presence of Christ in
the believer—is not to be understood as a new revelation in
which God talks to the believer directly, but it is mediated by
word and sacraments. Furthermore, *inhabitatio* does not grant

the believer any knowledge about the divine that goes beyond (or against) the revelation already codified in the bible and the sacraments administered by the church. The dwelling of God in the heart of the believer is, according to Arndt, the closest and most intimate connection between God and the believer; he compares this mystic unity with a marriage, "the unification of the Lord Christ with the faithful soul is caused by the spiritual marriage and wedding."[7] The spiritual marriage serves as a metaphor for the mystic unity established through the indwelling of Christ in the believer's heart.

Just as the beloved "lives" (metaphorically speaking) in the heart of the lover, Christ dwells in the hearts of the faithful. In Christmas hymns and religious poetry from the seventeenth and eighteenth centuries we find this idea expressed in the image of the human heart as the manger in which newborn Jesus makes his bed. Passion texts from the same time transform the metaphor and combine it with images from the passion narrative.

One of the later movements in the *St Matthew Passion* is the aria "Mache dich, mein Herze, rein" (Make yourself pure, my heart) (no. 65). The bass aria is part of a sequence of movements that begins with the narrative around the burial of Jesus. Joseph of Arimathea asks for permission to take Jesus' corpse. The biblical text mentions that this happened "am Abend," in the evening. The following two movements, both written by Picander, interpret the meaning of this verse. Both movements are set for bass. Even though it would be wrong to see these two movements as statements of one of the biblical characters, it is clear that Bach's choice was motivated by the fact that the actions in the biblical text were carried out by Joseph, a male character. The recitative and aria are a typological interpretation of Joseph's actions. The believer who meditates on the biblical text puts herself in the position of Joseph and asks: what does that which Joseph did mean for me today?

The first movement is an accompanied recitative for bass and strings. It begins with a meditation on the evening: Adam became aware of his sin when it got cool in the evening; in the evening the dove returned to Noah and carried an olive leaf. In other words, the evening is the time of original sin but it is also the time of salvation; and so the text rejoices: "O schöne Zeit! O Abendstunde!" (O lovely time! O evening hour!) and it continues, "Der Friedensschluß ist nun mit Gott gemacht, denn Jesus hat sein Kreuz vollbracht" (The peace treaty is now made with God, for Jesus has accomplished his cross). The focus shifts in the second half of the recitative, which asks for the significance of Joseph's wish to take the corpse and bury it. The soul is advised to do the same, and to desire the body of Christ: "Ach! Liebe Seele, bitte du, geh, lasse dir den toten Jesum schenken, o heilsames, o köstlich's Angedenken!" (Ah! dear soul, ask for the favor: go, let the death-stricken Jesus be given to you; o wholesome, o precious remembrance).

The following aria elaborates on the practical details: the human heart becomes the burial ground for Jesus. The first line asks for the purification of the heart, and then the text continues, "Ich will Jesum selbst begraben. Denn er soll nunmehr in mir für und für seine süße Ruhe haben. Welt, geht aus, laß Jesum ein!" (I wish to bury Jesus himself [inside my heart]. For within me shall he now, ever and ever, have his sweet rest. World, get out, let Jesus in). Christ is invited to dwell in the believer's heart. In order to do that, the believer has to purify his heart, drive out the world, and let Jesus enter.

Joseph of Arimathea becomes the model for the actions expected from the contemporary believer. The hermeneutical question is: what does it mean for me that Joseph buried

Christ? And the answer is: Joseph should be a model for every believer. Just as he buried Christ in the ground, the believers should bury Christ in their hearts. This image seems strange until we consider the theological context of the metaphor: burying Christ in the heart is nothing other than the idea of indwelling in the human heart, as described by Arndt. The metaphor of burying Christ in the heart describes the mystic unity between Christ and the believer; or in the language of the opening chorus, between bridegroom and bride.

The image has to be understood in a larger theological context. Johann Arndt had stressed that Christ comes into the believer's heart through the word and through the sacraments—especially the Eucharist. The text for the bass aria also has very strong, yet implicit, sacramental connotations. The Lord's Supper is the very place where the believer physically encounters the body of Christ and where she buries him inside of her body. We will see in a moment that this sacramental understanding of Christ's presence is of integral importance to the whole passion. Let us first have a closer look at the musical setting of the aria. Bach composes a movement for strings, oboi da caccia, and vocal bass. The instrumental introduction paints an almost bucolic image. Bach employs the style of a pastoral, to capture the calm tone of the aria. The flowing $\frac{12}{8}$ meter is typical of the pastoral. The almost static bass line at the beginning, the close parallel movement of the upper voices, and the use of reed instruments (here the two oboi da caccia), which were considered shepherds' instruments, all work to maintain this pastoral esthetic.

Bach transforms the images of nature the text of the accompagnato recitative had employed (Eden, Noah's dove) into music. The pastoral was the conventional device in baroque music to depict nature. At the same time, the movement also draws a connection to the very beginning of the *St Matthew Passion*. Bach uses the same meter as in the introductory movement of the passion, and even the static bass line is the same. Thus, the music with which the bridegroom was greeted hours before now returns when the bridegroom enters into the bride's heart to consummate the spiritual marriage. But the two movements are also significantly different from one another. The beginning of the passion was highly dramatic: the voices began in imitation and contrary motion, the harmonies were highly dissonant, and the texture sometimes disturbing. Now, after all has been accomplished, the tone of the music is calm. The voices proceed in parallel motion and the progression of the harmonies is much more straightforward.

The sad circumstances are visible only in a few instances. One example is the way Bach sets the word "begraben" (bury). A long descending line in the bass is combined with some unexpected harsh leaps; especially in measure 21, when the voice drops from A flat to B natural, two notes that do not belong to the key of B flat major in which the aria is written. The other instance is the rejection of the world: "Welt, geh aus" (World, get out), in measures 48–9. The wide leaps and the lack of a clear melodic line give the setting a stubborn, almost aggressive tone (example 5.3). However, the movement ends as it began: with the harmonious world of the pastoral-like ritornello.

The text of the *St Matthew Passion* has, as an underlying narrative, a love story. The bridegroom is greeted by the bride at the beginning of the piece. This aria marks the moment of the consummation of their mystic union. Other movements during the passion also allude to the highly emotional relationship between Christ and the believer. The first hymn, "Herzliebster Jesu" (no. 3), already marks the relationship with Christ as an emotional one, "Herzliebster Jesu, was hast du

Example 5.3: Bach, *St Matthew Passion* BWV 244/65, mm. 48–52

verbrochen" (Most beloved Jesus, what wrong have you committed). Later movements address Jesus as "Du lieber Heiland du" (You dear Savior) (no. 5), or sing "Blute nur, du liebes Herz!" (Bleed away, you loving heart!) (no. 8), and in a recitative, sung by the *Daughter of Zion*, we hear the text:

19. Recitative

Ach könnte meine Liebe dir, mein Heil, dein Zittern und dein Zagen vermindern oder helfen tragen, wie gerne blieb ich hier! (no. 19)	Oh, if only my love for you were able, my Salvation, to alleviate or help you to bear your trembling and your faintheartedness, how happily would I remain here!

The most explicit love song is the aria "Aus Liebe will mein Heiland sterben" (Out of love my Savior is willing to die) (no. 49). The text describes the reason for Christ's suffering. It is the expression of his love for mankind. This understanding of the passion is not unique to Picander or Bach. In fact, it is found frequently in theological treatises from the seventeenth and eighteenth centuries. We find traces of this understanding of the passion already in Luther's theology, but it is expanded by Lutheran theologians during the seventeenth century. Heinrich Müller, a popular preacher and author of devotional literature in the seventeenth century (some of his books were owned by Bach) writes:

Your Jesus loves you. Love seeks to be united with the beloved. In order to be united with you, Jesus has united himself with your flesh. ... He stands before your eyes as he hangs on the cross. He closes his mouth for you in order to kiss you. He stretches his arms to embrace you. He lets his hands be pierced to commit himself to you; lets his heart be opened with a spear to prepare a refuge for you; lets his feet be nailed to the wood to assure you that he is true, that he wishes to remain at your feet. Should you not hasten to your Jesus, like the bride to her bridegroom? His comforting mouth awaits you, you should turn your faithful mouth to him and wish: Ah, kiss me, my Jesus, with the kiss of your mouth. His arms are outstretched, you should take comfort here.... His heart is open: enter your nest, little bird; enter, dove, your rocky crevice.[8]

Images from the *Song of Songs* (bride and bridegroom; kisses of his mouth) are combined with images of Christ's wounded body. Johann Gerhard, another influential theologian from the seventeenth century, would summarize this thus, "namely, that we regard Christ's suffering as a clear mirror of his heartfelt, ardent love for us."[9] The love of the bridegroom for his bride manifests itself in his suffering for her: the greatest sacrifice of all for the beloved.

The theological treatises and sermons from the seventeenth century provide the context for the aria "Aus Liebe will mein Heiland sterben." The text names love as the reason for his suffering and also his sinlessness, "Von einer Sünde weiß er nichts." He dies in place of the believer: "So that eternal ruin, and the punishment of the Judgment, would not remain upon my soul." Bach's aria is an example of how the composer mirrors explicit and implicit theological aspects in his music. The aria simultaneously reflects the ideas of suffering and joy. The two oboi da caccia move in close parallel motion—a stylistic device baroque composers frequently employed to symbolize love. The solo flute that moves freely above the nasal sounds of the oboes is agitated, rhythmically highly complex, and covers a wide range. This is a different kind of love; not the harmonious unity of the two lovers as in the oboes (or as we saw earlier in the harmonious beginning of the bass aria) but an expression of longing and agitation. This impression of the music is confirmed when the soprano enters in measure 13: we have a long note on "Liebe" (love) expressing the longing for the beloved, which then turns into a searching melisma (example 5.4). The first time Bach presents the initial line of the text "Aus Liebe will mein Heiland sterben" he focuses on the aspect of love and not the dying. The word "Liebe" (love) occupies three measures while the setting of the word "sterben" (die) is only half a measure long. The focus is on God's love as the precondition for all that

Example 5.4: Bach, *St Matthew Passion* BWV 244/49, mm. 13–16

is happening. Or to use Johann Gerhard's words, "we regard Christ's suffering as a clear mirror of his heartfelt, ardent love for us."

Bach's musical depiction of love, however, is unsettling; something is wrong, missing, and incomplete: the aria does not have a foundation, no basso continuo. All the voices, the instruments as well as the soprano, are rather high and only rarely does the second oboe go below middle C. The texture of the movement indicates that this is not the joyful love we find in the *Song of Songs* or other love arias by Bach. The setting of the first line of the text already makes this clear. The third time Bach sets the line, the focus shifts from the word "Liebe" (love) to "sterben" (die), now highlighted with a longwinded melisma. It is different from the first melisma, which expressed longing and joy. This one is rhythmically broken: a dotted 8th note, a 16th note, a quarter note, syncopation, later another syncopation. All of this is combined with chromatic voice leading, expressing suffering. The melisma leads to a fermata in measure 24. The two instruments drop out and the unaccompanied voice of the soprano sounds all by itself, followed by a short moment of silence (example 5.5).

The shape of the soprano melody is one way Bach expresses the text. Even more striking, however, is the fact that the movement lacks a foundational bass line. Why did Bach leave out the instrumental bass voice? There are two reasons: one is simple and understandable without knowledge of baroque musical conventions. The lack of the bass voice gives the whole movement a feeling of incompleteness. Even without the text, we hear from the beginning the harmonious movement of the two oboes but we also sense that something is fundamentally wrong. The second reason is that the bass voice in the *St Matthew Passion* (and in most passions for that matter) represented Christ. The words of Christ are usually sung by the bass. Accordingly, when the instrumental bass voice drops out,

Example 5.5: Bach, *St Matthew Passion* BWV 244/49, mm. 21–24

we can understand this as another allusion to Christ's death. The love relationship the text talks about is only possible because Jesus has suffered and died.

Pain and Blood

We have to consider the other aspect of Christ's suffering highlighted in the *St Matthew Passion*: the pain and the extensive treatment of Christ's blood, wounds, and pain: "Bleed away, you loving heart," "O agony," "He suffers all the sorrows of Hell." How does this fascination with cruelty and suffering fit with the love songs?

The emphasis on Christ's love and his pain are not contradictory, but intrinsically intertwined. The emphasis on the cruelty of Christ's suffering simultaneously highlights the greatness of the love that is revealed through this suffering. The focus on Christ's wounds has a pedagogical purpose. The "presentation of cruelty [is] intended to excite horror and sympathy."[10] Eighteenth-century theologian Johann Jacob Rambach (1693–1735) would express it thus: the believer should meditate on the passion "so that the tears and sighs of Jesus Christ might be a fruitful seed, out of which many tears of repentance and holy sighs might arise and grow," and, he continues, "However, this love offers up no tears but those that flow from the pure wellspring of love ... No tears must come to your eyes but tears of love."[11] In other words, we might be shocked by the suffering of Christ, but our tears should not be a reaction to the suffering of a human being. Rather, tears should be a reaction to the love that is expressed in this suffering. Pain and love cannot be separated, but are two sides of the same coin. The description of pain is intended to move and convert the listener.

Communion

The mystic unity of the bridegroom, Christ, and the bride—
the *inhabitatio Christi*—takes place in the believer's heart and
it is mediated through word and sacraments. The meditation
on Christ's passion (with its emphasis on love and the pedagogical description of Christ's suffering) is exemplified in how
the words of arias like "Mache dich, mein Herze, rein" and
"Aus Liebe will mein Heiland sterben" mediate Christ's presence. The first of the above mentioned arias in particular also
has a subtext that alludes to the Eucharist, the sacramental
presence of Christ. In fact, there is a very strong connection
between love, Christ's suffering, and the Eucharist in Bach's
own theological tradition as well.

Martin Luther interprets the Lord's Supper as a sacrament
of love.[12] Similarly, seventeenth-century preacher Heinrich
Müller writes: "God's love does not content itself with giving
you his blessing through his Word, but seeks to give his very
self to you. That is perfect love ... Love can reach no higher
than to give you its own flesh and blood, and allow you to eat
and drink of it."[13] And Müller later continues:

Holy Communion is a signature in Christ's blood, assuring
you of his love. Therefore it is given in the form of
food and drink, so that he embodies and plants his love in
our heart with his blood. We eat and drink his love; it
becomes our manna and wine, our strong refreshment and
pleasure. This love transcends all human thought and
should rightly penetrate and wound every heart ... Because
Christ loves us with all his strength in perfect love, he
wants to be united with us so that he may become
one body and spirit with us, and we with him. Therefore

he gave us Holy Communion in the form of food and drink.[14]

Christ's passion is the deepest demonstration of Christ's love and the Lord's Supper is the celebration and reminder of this love. This is confirmed by the way Bach and Picander set the words of institution in the *St Matthew Passion*.

The words of institution of the Eucharist are interpreted in a sequence of three distinct movements. The first recitative reports the biblical story, followed by meditative responses in an accompanied recitative, sung by the soprano, and a soprano aria. I will begin my analysis with the accompagnato recitative; we will return to the biblical text in a moment. The accompagnato recitative (no. 12) features the soprano, accompanied by two oboi d'amore. The text contains some of the familiar metaphors of mystical love: the heart swims in tears because Jesus (the beloved) takes leave. But the believer is still glad because of the "testament," his flesh and blood which are given in the Lord's Supper; and all of this has happened, as the final lines point out, because he loves his followers until the end. If we read the text of the recitative backwards, we see the Lutheran orthodox understanding of communion: God loves the world so much that he gives himself and, even though we might cry, we are consoled because he gives himself in flesh and blood. In other words: the Lord's Supper is the manifestation of divine love.

Consequently, Bach's setting features some characteristics that we are used to seeing in love duets from the eighteenth century. First of all, the close parallel motion in the two oboes: there is almost no measure where they do not move in parallel thirds and sixths. The rapid motive in triplets, on the other hand, that accompanies the entire recitative, musically "paints" the flowing of the tears (example 5.6). In the instrumental accompaniment, Bach combines the tears with the idea of love. A listener in Bach's Leipzig would also have understood the instrumentation of the movement as something love-related. The two oboi d'amore, love oboes, are instruments Bach (and his contemporaries) used frequently when they set texts that revolved around the subject of love. The last line of the recitative text provides Bach with the key for his under-standing of the whole text, "he loves them until the end." Love musically permeates the entire movement even before the text explicitly mentions it.

The following aria (no. 13) has the same instrumenta-tion—again two oboi d'amore and soprano—and the text continues the train of thought begun in the previous recitative. "Ich will dir mein Herze schenken" (I will give my heart to you). It is a typical line from a love song (even in the

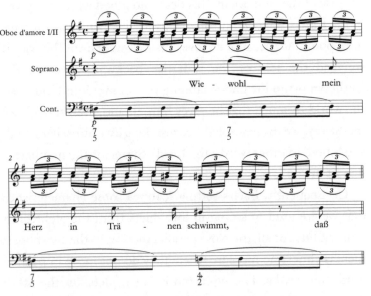

Example 5.6: Bach, *St Matthew Passion* BWV 244/12, mm. 1–2

eighteenth century), here addressed to Jesus, the bridegroom from the *Song of Songs*. But the bride not only gives her heart (and it is not by accident that the aria is sung by the soprano, who often personifies the spiritual bride in Bach's music), but she invites the Savior to sink into the heart: "Senke dich, mein Heil, hinein" (Sink into it, my Salvation). We understand that this metaphor denotes again the *inhabitatio Christi*, the dwelling of Christ in the believer's heart. This, as any eighteenth-century Lutheran theologian would point out, is given through the Eucharist. Or to quote Johann Arndt again:

> In the words and in the holy sacraments is laid down the true memory of the name of God. That is why he is unified with us through the word and the sacrament; which was confirmed by the Savior through the beautiful and lovely saying: He who loves me will keep my word and my father will love him and we will come to him and dwell with him.[15]

Bach's setting is a beautiful, highly optimistic aria in G major. The two oboi d'amore engage in little dialogues and move in parallel motion—just as we would expect in a secular love duet. The soprano follows the lead of the two instruments and sings her text with an ascending motive, breaking out in a joyful sigh on the word "heart," and descending on the three-fold repetition of the word "senke" (sink). From a theological perspective it is clear why Bach and Picander elaborate so extensively on the human heart and on love as an interpretation of the words of institution. We can also see that Bach makes extensive use of motives, textures, and intervals, the musical toolbox of a baroque composer employed for a text associated with love.

Let us now turn back to the setting of the words of institution. As usual, Bach differentiates between the words of the evangelist and the words of Christ, with the latter being accompanied by a string ensemble, while the former are only accompanied by the "dry" basso continuo. The strings serve as a "halo" for the words of Christ, but they also give the composer a wider range of harmonic and motivic possibilities. The way Bach sets the words of institution is interesting. If we compare it to the previous setting of the words of Christ in the passion, where he asks his disciples to go into the city to find a room to celebrate Passover, the setting is not much different from the part of the evangelist, except that Bach uses the string-halo (extended chords played by the higher string instruments). This is different in the setting of the words of institution. The meter switches into triple time and the melodic line is much more song-like than the declamatory recitative sung by the evangelist. We also see that the vocal bass and the basso continuo move in harmonious parallel motion. And even where Bach gives up the parallel movement of the two voices, he creates as many harmonious intervals as possible between the vocal and instrumental basses. The strings in the upper voices add further harmonious chords, often in parallel progression as well, between two or more of the voices. The result is a beautiful, harmonious setting of the words of institution. But it is more than that. The highly melodic, diatonic voice leading, the parallel movement between two voices (which is accentuated by the unusual fact that two bass voices move in parallel), and the sometimes dialogic interplay between the vocal and instrumental bass voices, are typical features of love duets at this time. Bach sets the words of institution as a love song. Not as a dramatic love dialogue between bridegroom and bride, but more as a general representation of the idea of love—love as a principle that is at the core of Christ's passion and of the Eucharist. The two following movements, which I discussed before, show that this indeed was Bach and Picander's understanding of the Lord's Supper.[16]

Two Endings

I will end this chapter with a few words about the final movements of the two parts of the passion. Before the intermission (or, for Bach's listeners in Leipzig, before the sermon), we hear a large-scale hymn setting: "O Mensch, bewein dein Sünde groß" (O humankind, bewail your great sin). It is a magnificent example of Bach's hymn settings: it begins with a long instrumental introduction, almost an instrumental concerto by itself, before the voices enter with a highly embellished and polyphonic setting of the Protestant passion hymn. Bach's listeners in 1727 would have heard a different piece, a simple hymn setting with another text. The movement that is now part of the passion was originally composed for a revised version of the St John Passion and performed for the first time in 1725. Bach would later revise the St John Passion again and the setting found its way into the St Matthew Passion in 1736. Its dimensions and instrumentation provide an excellent balance with the first movement of the piece. Even some musical features in the two pieces are similar: a long extended note (organ point) in the bass on E, and a slowly ascending motive in the upper voices. If we did not know that these two movements were originally conceived for different occasions, we would probably assume that they were written as a perfect frame for the first part of the St Matthew Passion.

This brings us back to the very beginning of the passion— the exordium, the "headline" in the first movement. Picander writes a dialogue between the *Daughter of Zion* and the *Believers*, awaiting the bridegroom who is about to be slaughtered like a lamb. The movement, as I said earlier, sets the stage for an understanding of the passion as a story about Christ's love and of the suffering as an expression of this love. *Daughter of Zion* and the *Believers* are set as two independent ensembles, engaging in a dialogue; but Bach adds another layer. A third choir sings a well-known hymn, "O Lamm Gottes unschuldig" (O Lamb of God). The hymn is a familiar passion chorale but it is also one of the German versions of the *Agnus Dei*, the invocation of the "Lamb of God," which has its place in the liturgy of the Lord's Supper. The hymn infuses the opening chorus with a reference to the Eucharist. Considering how closely related the themes of love, suffering, and Eucharist were at this time, it is understandable why Bach adds the hymn. It highlights the sacramental presence of Christ in the believer, which is then later elaborated on in the scene with the institution of the Eucharist, but also towards the end of the passion when the body of Christ is finally buried in the believer's heart.

The second part of the *St Matthew Passion* ends with another large-scale choral movement. Like the very first movement, Bach composes a piece for two choirs, *Daughter of Zion* and the *Believers*, but instead of a dialogue, the two groups sing the same text, a lullaby for the dead Jesus:

68. Zion and the Believers

Wir setzen uns mit Tränen nieder	With tears we sit down
Und rufen dir im Grabe zu:	And call to you in the grave:
Ruhe sanfte, sanfte ruh! . . .	You rest in peace, in peace rest! . . .

Bach sets this farewell song as a calm lullaby: a slowly rocking triple meter, flowing musical lines in the instruments and the voices, and a simple, song-like texture in the vocal setting. The music is calm, but not because the listener knows that Easter Sunday is just two days away—that would probably be an anachronistic, modern interpretation. Rather, the death was necessary for the forgiveness of sins (as the final hymn of the first half pointed out). Jesus has died because of his pure love for humankind, as the very first movement of the *St Matthew Passion* had announced. The use of a lilting lullaby also alludes to the Lutheran understanding of death as sleep, as the end of the *St John Passion* had already highlighted: "Be fully at peace, you holy bones, which I will no longer bewail; be fully at peace and bring also me to this place!" (*St John Passion*, no. 39) The nineteenth-century reviewer I quoted at the beginning of this essay described the *St Matthew Passion* as a "depressing ... iteration of grief." As a setting of the death of Christ, the composition has to be full of grief. However, this grief, and even the sometimes quite graphic descriptions of Jesus' agony and his bloody wounds, serve a pedagogical purpose as they highlight the understanding of the passion as an expression of divine love. Even though the narrative stops short of Easter morning, the mood at the end of the *St Matthew Passion* is calm, and not depressing at all.

CHAPTER SIX

SEEING AND UNDERSTANDING
The Oratorios for Easter and Ascension
BWV 249 and 11

Oh, please stay, my dearest life (BWV 11/4)

An Inquiry into the understanding, pleasant and useful.

Since it is the Understanding that sets Man above the
rest of sensible Beings, and gives him all the Advantage
and Dominion, which he has over them; it is certainly a
Subject, even for its Nobleness, worth our Labour to
inquire into. The Understanding, like the Eye, whilst it
makes us see, and perceive all other Things, takes no notice
of it self: And it requires Art and Pains to set it at a distance
and make it its own Object. But whatever be the Difficulties,
that lie in the way of this Enquiry; whatever it be that
keeps us so much in the Dark to ourselves; sure I am that
all the Light we can let in upon our Minds, all the
Acquaintance we can make with our own Understandings,
will not only be very pleasant, but bring us great Advantage,
in directing our Thoughts in the search of other Things.[1]

This is the famous opening paragraph of John Locke's *Essay
Concerning Human Understanding*, published in 1690. Locke's
treatise was one of the founding documents of empiricism in

the seventeenth century. The trust that knowledge could be derived primarily from sensory experience put the human—as the observer—at the center of concepts like perception, knowledge, and eventually the understanding of the world as it is. This idea was based on the assumption that the human mind was able to perceive reality and to evaluate it rationally. Locke did limit his claims by conceding that there were things that were incomprehensible to men (which included divine providence); however, these theories essentially opened the doors to a secularized world view.

Johann Sebastian Bach's two smaller oratorios for the feasts of Easter and Ascension can be heard as explorations of the questions of seeing and understanding; or—to employ philosophical terms from the 1700s—of empiricism and rationalism. One of the crucial philosophical questions of the time was, how could the world be understood? Should it be by simply referring to traditions, by reasoning, or by observing the world and drawing appropriate individual conclusions? This, in turn, could lead to a perception of the world that contradicted, or at least challenged, tradition, including the Christian tradition. John Locke's essay is just one example of this view. Another one is the philosophy of Gottfried Wilhelm Leibnitz (1645–1716), who challenged Locke's empiricism and emphasized the imperfection of perception by raising the importance of the human mind in the construction of reality, while still placing the human mind at the center of the intellectual universe.

The philosopher Christian Wolff (1679–1759), was the most influential voice in this discourse during Johann Sebastian Bach's time. Wolff's rationalist views were harshly criticized by Lutheran orthodox, as well as Pietist, theologians—the two major camps in German Protestantism in the first half of the eighteenth century. For Wolff, expanding the ideas of

Leibnitz, perception of the world is the basis of knowledge, but rational reasoning is required for true understanding. Wolff states in his book, *Vernünftige Gedancken von den Kräfften des menschlichen Verstandes und ihrem richtigen Gebrauche* (1713),[2] his view of the relationship between empiricism (the perception of reality) and rationalism (the understanding of this perceived reality in the human mind):

Da nun die Sinnen uns zu Gedancken von Dingen / die ausser uns sind / veranlassen ... so bringen sie uns einen Begriff derselben bey. Solcher gestalt bekommen wir durch das Sehen einen Begriff von dem Lichte und den Farben; durch das Hören von dem Schalle; durch das Fühlen von dem / was weich oder harte ist; durch das Riechen von Geruch und Gestanck / durch das Schmecken von süssem und saurem ...[3]

As the senses enable us to think about things that are external to us ... they do teach us the idea of these things. In that way, we get an idea of light and colors by seeing, of sound by hearing; we get an idea of what is soft and what hard by feeling, of odor and stench by smelling; of sweet and sour by tasting ...

By evaluating this external information, the human mind is capable of understanding the world and Wolff differentiates between those things we do know and those we "just believe:"

Durch den Glauben verstehe ich den Beyfall / den man einem Satze giebet umb eines anderen Zeugnisses Willen ... wenn ich es vor wahr halte / das ist / wenn ich dencke es sey geschehen; so glaube ich es ...

By 'belief' I mean the agreement with a sentence based on someone else's testimony ... if I deem something to be true, that is, if I think that something had happened, then I believe it ...

Der Glaube erstreckt sich also nur	Belief only refers to things that
auff Dinge / die geschehen sind	have happened or that shall
oder geschehen sollen. Denn die	happen. Because all other things
übrigen Sachen lassen sich	can be proven and thus can be
erweisen / und also kan man sie	known.
wissen.[4]	

Like Locke, Wolff makes sure that his readers do not mistake him for an atheist and he stresses that divine revelation is excluded from this paradigm. But again, it is only gradually removed from a non-metaphysical understanding of the world. Partly in reaction to accusation of being an atheist, Wolff published his *Theologia Naturalis* in 1736/7. The book came out at about the same time as Bach's oratorios were composed (1734–8). The philosophical treatise attempts to reconcile faith and divine revelation on the one side and rationality and empiricism on the other.[5] However, the result was essentially the victory of the human mind over pre-Enlightenment religiosity.

Johann Sebastian Bach's oratorios, while not conceived as theological or philosophical treatises, are embedded in these highly contested discourses by interacting with popular topics such as seeing, understanding, rationality, and divine providence. The oratorios have to be understood within the larger theological and philosophical landscape of the 1730s, even if the librettos were not intended as philosophical texts. They exist contemporaneously and inevitably reflect that zeitgeist. The libretto for the *Christmas Oratorio* from 1734/5 had already taken a rather clear anti-rationalist stance, declaring that God and the miracle of the incarnation could only be understood with the help of divine revelation ('divine light') and not through human reasoning. The oratorios for Easter

and Ascension return to this subject: what do we see? How do
we perceive reality? Where do we look for Jesus Christ? How
do we interpret what we see? In the *Easter Oratorio* it is the
women who find the empty "Schweißtuch" (sudarium, shroud)
and who criticize the men for not seeing and for not
understanding:

4. Recitative

O kalter Männer Sinn!	O cold disposition of menfolk!
Wo ist die Liebe hin,	Where has the love gone
Die ihr dem Heiland schuldig seid?	That you all owe the Savior?

In the *Ascension Oratorio* the disciples look up to the sky,
following with their eyes the ascending Jesus. Now, two angels
admonish the men to look down to earth if they want to find
Jesus. Where is the divine to be found? Do the eyes suffice to
"see" or do we need more than empirical observation? We will
return to these questions later in our discussion of these two
oratorios.

Why Oratorios?

Johann Sebastian Bach's interest in the genre 'oratorio' intensi-
fied quite suddenly. The famous opera composer and music
director at the court in Dresden, Johann Adolph Hasse, had
begun performing oratorios on Good Friday 1734. At this
time in his life, Bach was fascinated by the musical life at the
Saxon court. After his attempts to win the honorary title of
court composer at the Saxon court had been unsuccessful (at
least for several years), he attempted to model his own position
in Leipzig after the court in the Saxon capital. One of the
results was a trilogy of oratorios for the major feast days:

Christmas, Easter, and Ascension.⁶ While the *Christmas Oratorio* is the most famous piece from this trilogy, the two smaller pieces are fascinating and quite effective compositions as well.

The three oratorios, as we have discussed in the opening chapter of this book, are designed to be performed in the mass liturgy on the morning of their specific feast days. They reflect on the readings of each particular day and provide an interpretation of these readings, a precursor to the scriptural exegesis of the sermon. In other words, they can be viewed as musical sermons on the gospel texts for the specific day.⁷ We see Bach again as a storyteller. But as in the *Christmas Oratorio*, contemplating the meaning of the story is more important than the dramatic narrative. We have already seen in the *Magnificat* BWV 243 that Bach shows a keen sense for the dramatic and expressive potential of the texts he has to set, without being overtly operatic or dramatic. Accordingly, the two oratorios deal with this "drama" in very distinct ways.

Complex Histories

Like the *Christmas Oratorio* from 1734/5, the two smaller oratorios have a complex history. The earliest version of the *Easter Oratorio* BWV 249 dates from 1725, long before Bach called it an oratorio. On Easter Sunday 1725, two days after the premiere performance of his revised version of the *St John Passion*, Bach performed his Easter cantata *Kommt, eilet und laufet* BWV 249. The piece was unusual as it did not quote the original biblical text but presented the narrative of the discovery of the empty grave on Easter morning through a conversation between the four characters, Peter, John, Mary Magdalene, and Mary the mother of James. The style is very close to modern oratorios, but interestingly enough, Bach did not call the piece an oratorio.

The music for this cantata was a parody. Bach had originally written it for the shepherds' cantata *Entfliehet, verschwindet, entweichet, ihr Sorgen* BWV 249a, composed for the birthday of Herzog Christian of Sachsen-Weissenfels on February 23, 1725. The libretto for the secular cantata was provided by Christian Friedrich Henrici (called Picander) and 'enacts' dialogues between the shepherds, Menalcas and Damoetus, and the shepherdesses, Doris and Sylvia. The secular cantata resembles a little operatic scene, a feature that would have been easily recognized by the audience, as the court in Weissenfels had a longstanding tradition of opera performances.[8] A few weeks after the performance of the secular cantata, Bach revived the piece to adapt it to a new function as an Easter cantata.[9] Given the proximity of the original context for its composition and parody, it is even possible that Bach had already planned to use the music on Easter morning 1725.

Bach returned to the music from 1725 a bit more than a decade later. In 1734/5 he had composed the *Christmas Oratorio* and around 1738 (maybe even slightly earlier) he looked for a piece for Easter Sunday. If we define the oratorio as the "sacred sister" of the opera, the dialogical structure of *Kommt, eilet und laufet* could almost be considered an oratorio. However, Bach's oratorio concept in the 1730s was different. It is this version from the 1730s that Bach now explicitly labeled 'oratorio.' He favored a contemplative oratorio—as he found it in the works by his favorite composer, Gottfried Heinrich Stölzel[10]—a form Bach had already realized in his *Christmas Oratorio*. He revised his earlier piece, eliminating the names of the four protagonists. The first vocal movement, while still featuring the same text and music, was given a different meaning. Instead of being a dialogue between the two male disciples, it is now a general invitation to hasten towards the grave of Jesus:

3. Duet

Kommt, eilet und laufet, ihr flüchtigen Füße,	Come, hurry and run, you nimble feet;
Erreichet die Höhle, die Jesum bedeckt!	Reach the cavern that sheltered Jesus!
Lachen und Scherzen	Laughing and jesting
Begleitet die Herzen,	Attend our hearts,
Denn unser Heil ist auferweckt.	For our Salvation is raised.

The same applies to the other movements of the *Easter Oratorio*. By eliminating the names of the protagonists, the paraphrases of the biblical texts are transformed into meditations on the biblical narrative that had been read within the liturgy immediately before the performance of the cantata/ oratorio. In the 1740s, Bach revised the work again. At this time, oratorios were further from his mind. He took the final step of turning the Easter piece into a "regular" cantata, expanding the dialogue between the disciples from the Easter story into a four-part chorus.

The *Ascension Oratorio* BWV 11 has a more straightforward history. However, it has its complexities as well. Like the *Christmas Oratorio*, the *Ascension Oratorio* uses parodies from several earlier secular cantatas (see Table 2 in Appendix B). Not only were the movements of the *Ascension Oratorio* derived from different sources, but the biblical narrative is a pasticcio as well. The words are assembled from the stories about the ascension of Jesus from the Gospel according to Luke, and Luke's Acts of the Apostles. The texts, however, were not assembled by Bach's (unknown) librettist. Instead, these texts can already be found in the *Evangelienharmonie* (Gospel Harmony), by Johannes Bugenhagen (1485–1558).[11] The text from Bugenhagen's *Evangelienharmonie* serves as the backbone for the oratorio. Interpretations of the narrative are included in the form of accompagnato recitatives, arias, and chorales—in a similar manner to the *Christmas Oratorio*.

Easter Oratorio BWV 249

Easter Sunday is a celebratory feast, and Bach's *Easter Oratorio* thus begins with a festive opening. Instead of an opening chorus, we hear two instrumental movements before the voices enter in movement 3. While some earlier cantatas by Bach begin with an instrumental opening movement, it is unusual that we have two movements (a fast movement followed by a slow one) before the vocalists begin. The unusual format is due to the secular model Bach used here for his *Easter Oratorio*.

The opening movement, though exclusively instrumental, projects a festive and celebratory character. In 1725, Bach's contemporary, the poet and theologian Gottfried Ephraim Scheibel (1696–1759), published a collection of cantata libretti. While none of the texts were set by Bach, the text for the first chorus in Scheibel's Easter cantata nicely captures the mood of the first instrumental movement in Bach's oratorio: trumpets, drums, and strings praise the resurrection of Christ:

Scheibel (1725)

Stoßt an die Trompeten laßt die Lieder erschallen,	Blow the trumpets, let your songs sound,

Beym Pochen der Paucken und	During the beating of the drums
Rauschen der Säyten,	and the humming of the strings,
Besinget die frölich und	Sing about the joyful and holy
heilge Zeiten,	times,
Daß Jesus gesieget, die	When Jesus won and the enemies
Feinde gefallen.[12]	fell.

Bach scholars have convincingly suggested that the first two movements of the *Easter Oratorio* might have originated as an independent instrumental concerto (not unlike the famous *Brandenburg Concertos* Bach had composed a few years prior). It is even possible that the third movement, which now features the singers, was originally the third movement of that concerto and that Bach expanded it later for the cantata.

Whatever the history of the movements might have been, within the context of the *Easter Oratorio* they create an interesting sequence of moods and affects. The first movement sets the celebratory stage. The different groups of instruments engage in a dialogue: trumpets and drums, oboes, and the string section play together in massive tutti blocks and then alternate in a spirited conversation. Every time the trumpets enter, the first trumpet dominates, giving the movement an exceedingly jubilant character.

The second movement transports the listener from this exuberant state into a more subdued mood. The oboe (in a later version replaced by a flute) plays elegiac lines over simple chords in the strings. Bach did not compose the movement as program music; however, it is possible to hear the oboe solo as a depiction of the desolation of the disciples on Easter morning. We find a similar oboe movement at the beginning of Bach's well-known cantata, *Weinen, Klagen, Sorgen, Zagen* BWV 12 (Weeping, lamenting, grieving, trembling), where it precedes a vocal movement that bemoans the suffering of those who follow Christ in his path of suffering.[13] In both cases, the plaintive and sad oboe lines create a mood of longing and mourning. This mood, however, changes again in the third movement of the oratorio: we are back in the celebratory realm of the opening sinfonia; trumpets and timpani dominate the sound, and the two male singers encourage one another to hasten to the grave because Christ has risen: "Come, hurry and run, you nimble feet; reach the cavern that sheltered Jesus!"

When Bach revised the piece in the late 1730s, he eliminated the names of the protagonists. What remains is a movement that encourages the listener to "spiritually" hasten to the grave and to witness the resurrection by meditating on the biblical narrative. This revision takes care of a logical problem within the libretto of the 1725 version. While the opening movement talks about the resurrection as a *fait accompli*, the following movements tell the story as if the disciples did not know that Christ had already risen. They contemplate how to embalm the body of Jesus, and wonder how the massive stone in front of the grave could be removed. The logical order is out of balance. This burden is lighter if the singers just meditate on the gospel reading instead of enacting it.

The first vocal movement encourages the listeners to (spiritually) hasten to the grave themselves. The next movement, a recitative for the four singers, deals with the question of how the grave should be approached. We are back to the question I discussed at the beginning of this chapter, the relationship between empirical observation and rational reasoning. The two female voices chide the men for their "kalter Männer Sinn" (cold disposition), lacking the love they owe to the Savior; and the second female voice adds, "ein schwaches Weib muß euch beschämen" (a weak woman has to put you all to shame). It had been a recurring theme in sermons and devotional texts from the seventeenth and early eighteenth centuries to point out the exceptional fact that women (who were still considered intellectually weaker) were the first to witness the resurrection. The seventeenth-century theologian Heinrich Müller wrote in his *Evangelische Schluß-kett* (a sermon collection owned by Bach):[14]

Wie verachtet sind doch die Weiber für den Männern! Aber das Verachtete erwählet GOtt, und thut durch kleine Mittel grosse Dinge, daß die Ehre seines Namens desto grösser sey.[15]

How despised are women in comparison to men! But God chooses what is despised and by small means he does great things, so that the glory of his name might be even greater.

A few movements later, in recitative no. 6, the two men again fail to comprehend the meaning of the empty grave. They see the "Gruft" (the grave) but anxiously ask: "Wo aber wird mein Heiland sein?" (But where might my Savior be?). In their cold, masculine empiricism, the male disciples fail to comprehend the meaning. Only the women are able to see and understand: "Er ist vom Tode auferweckt! Wir trafen einen Engel an" (He is raised from the dead! We met an angel). Peter needs a divine intervention and the loving perspective of the women to understand what he is seeing: "Hier seh ich mit Vergnügen das Schweißtuch abgewickelt liegen" (I am pleased to see here the sudarium lying unwrapped). Peter observes the facts, but his interpretation is guided by faith, not solely by logical reasoning. Heinrich Müller writes in his Easter sermon in a similar vein when he states:

Anderswo musten die Apostel vom Kinde lernen, wie sie solten ins Himmelreich kommen; hie sich von den Weibern unterrichten lassen, daß Christus aufferstanden sey; von den Weibern, denen sonst das öffentliche Predigen in der Kirchen verboten. So ist die Weißheit dieser Welt zur Thorheit gemacht worden, auf daß erkannt würde, daß die Göttliche Thorheit weiser sey, dann die Menschen sind.[16]

At another place the apostles had to learn from a child how to enter the Kingdom of Heaven; here, they have to be taught by women that Christ is risen. [They learn it] from women who are otherwise prohibited from publicly preaching in church. Thus, the wisdom of the world is turned into foolishness in order to show that divine foolishness is [still] wiser than mankind.

Reasoning, 'wisdom of the world,' is cold. Bach expresses this coldness with a shockingly harsh and chilling chord at the beginning of the first recitative. We have just left the lavish and exuberant sounds of the first vocal movement, when the basso continuo plays a diminished seventh chord, on top of which the alto sings her criticism of the cold male disposition (or mind). The soprano aria "Seele, deine Spezereien" (Soul, your spices) provides a counter model, a highly emotional aria that describes how the soul should not be embalmed with myrrh, but it should rather be crowned with laurel. The aria is about ornamentation, embellishment, and eventually about beauty: the beauty of the soul that opens itself for Christ. Beauty is not rational, not even functional. It transcends function. The highly ornate and wide-ranging flute (or violin) solo that opens the aria is a case in point. The rhythmic variety of the musical ideas, including wide-ranging lines, and a turn from regular 16th notes to 16th triplets, is an expression of joy, but it also echoes the type of exuberance that the text of the aria evokes (example 6.1).

Example 6.1: Bach, *Easter Oratorio* BWV 249/5, mm. 1–17

Do the cold men understand this? Not yet. What follows is a recitative in which the women have to teach the men to interpret the empty grave. Only then is the tenor (in the original version it is Peter) able to identify the sudarium (shroud) as proof for the resurrection.[17] Then the tenor sings an aria with a beautiful meditation on the meaning of the sudarium: Jesus' shroud turns into a signifier for the hope that the pain of death will only be sleep. The shroud will refresh the believer in death and it will wipe the tears off his face. The theological idea that stands in the background here is that death is but sleep. This concept figures prominently in a Lutheran theology of death. After the Reformation had rejected the medieval theology of Purgatory, this had to be replaced with a new answer to the question: where do we go after death? The answer was: death is just sleep and we will be woken up by

God at the end of time. Heinrich Müller writes in his Easter sermon:

Er ist auferstanden. Der Tod hat ihn nieder gelegt, er hat sich aber wieder aufgerichtet. Er hatte sich im Grabe niedergelegt zu schlaffen, ist aber schon wieder aufgewacht. Sein Tod ist ein kurtzer Schlaff. Und unser Tod durch seinen Todes-Schlaff in einen Schlaff verwandelt. Wir schlaffen ein, wir schlaffen aus, und wachen wieder auf.[18]	He has risen. Death had laid him [to rest] but he has stood up again. He had laid down in the grave to sleep but he has already woken up again. His death is a short sleep. By his death-sleep, our death was [also] turned into merely sleep. We fall asleep, we sleep for a while, and then we wake up again.

A well-known example of this concept is the penultimate movement of Johann Sebastian Bach's *St John Passion*. The text of the movement reads:

39. Chorus

Ruht wohl, ihr heiligen Gebeine,	Be fully at peace, you holy bones,
Die ich nun weiter nicht beweine,	Which I will no longer bewail;
Ruht wohl und bringt auch mich zur Ruh!	Be fully at peace and bring also me to his peace!
Das Grab, so euch bestimmet ist	The grave—which is appointed to you
Und ferner keine Not umschließt,	And from now on no distress will enclose—
Macht mir den Himmel auf und schließt die Hölle zu.	Opens Heaven to me and closes hell.

Just by glancing at the text, some readers might have been reminded of the music Bach composed to set the words: a lilting triple meter, smooth lines, slow-moving harmonies, soothing melodic gestures. In other words, Bach composes a lullaby that underscores the idea of sleep we find in the text (see Chapter Four). In the *Easter Oratorio*, Bach sets the text in the form of a lullaby as well. The basso continuo plays a static yet pulsating foundation, the second violin and the second recorder proceed in slow-moving 8th notes, while the first recorder and the first violin play lilting and repetitive 16th-note figurations. We can almost hear the rocking cradle. The movement was, of course, part of the shepherds' cantata BWV 249a, where it was sung by the shepherd Menalcas to lull his sheep to sleep. We see that the musical idiom was the same both in the sacred and the secular contexts, which further suggests that Bach's listeners would have immediately identified the aria as a soothing lullaby.

The new text was written so that it could go perfectly with the music. The following musical example shows the beginning of the tenor part. The sweetness of the beginning is expressed in the smooth 8th-note line, then a disturbance of the rhythmic flow enters on "Todeskummer" (death's grief, measure 14). But this disturbance is only temporary. In the following measure, the voice returns to the soothing 8th-note motive and then comes to a long rest on the word "Schlummer" (slumber) (example 6.2). Listeners might also be reminded of the "Schlafe" aria in Bach's *Christmas Oratorio* (movement 19), which uses similar musical stereotypes, including the extended note on the word for sleep (see Chapter Three).

The hope that Christ will wipe away the tears at the end of time might be an eventual consolation. But, as we have seen in the chapter on the *Christmas Oratorio*, piety in Bach's time paid particular attention to the immediate presence of Christ in the believer's heart, not only at some time in the future but

Example 6.2: Bach, *Easter Oratorio* BWV 249/7, mm. 13–18

now. The recitative "Indessen seufzen wir" (Meanwhile we sigh) expresses a desire for the presence of Christ. The two women sing sigh-like motives in mostly homophonic, parallel motion. The recitative expresses the longing most poignantly. The following alto aria explores this longing further. Bach combines several ingredients he frequently uses to express emotional longing for Jesus: the obbligato instrumental part is played by the oboe d'amore, the "love oboe," an oboe with a particularly sweet sound which we find frequently in Bach's arias that talk about love and longing. The vocal soloist is the alto, which is also Bach's preferred voice for arias that express the longing for the presence of Jesus. We find several arias of this type in the *Christmas Oratorio*. Here in the Easter piece, the alto searches for Jesus, whom her soul loves. She asks him to come since her heart was lonely and sad without him. As for every lover, this cannot happen fast enough and thus the alto urges Jesus to come "geschwinde" (quickly). The 16th notes in the opening ritornello already allude to this urgency.

A particularly striking and moving moment in the aria is Bach's musical depiction of the soul's loneliness (measures 68–71). The instruments drop out and leave the singer all by herself (or himself, as in Bach's times the part would have been sung by the male singer) (example 6.3). In the end, however, joy over the resurrection wins over the fear of loneliness. After a bass recitative expressing exactly this joy, the *Easter Oratorio* ends with a celebratory choral movement, which brings back the full ensemble with trumpets and timpani and again presents the instrumental groups in a vivid dialogue. The text praises the divine victory over hell and Satan. Like in other pieces we have discussed earlier in this book, the final movement balances out the beginning by employing the same instrumentation. The movement celebrates the risen Christ as the "Lion of Judah," who victoriously defeats his enemies. We are reminded of the aria "Es ist vollbracht" (It is accomplished) from the *St John Passion* (no. 30), with its central section that interpreted the death of the "Hero from Judah" at the cross as a sign of his victory. And Heinrich Müller, in one of his Easter sermons, interprets the earthquake at Christ's death and writes:

Example 6.3: Bach, *Easter Oratorio* BWV 249/9, mm. 68–72

Die Erde hatte Ursach zu beben, indem der GOTT, der sie gemacht hatte, mit solcher Macht sein eigen Fleisch … in ihrem Bauche wieder forderte. Ursach hatte die Erde zu beben, denn der Löwe vom Stamm Juda hatte überwunden. Wann die Sieges-Helden im Triumph einziehen, so donnert man ihnen mit Carthaunen

The earth had a reason to tremble as God, who had made the earth, demanded with all his power … from its belly his own flesh. The earth had a reason to tremble because the Lion from the tribe of Judah had succeeded [victoriously]. When the victorious heroes enter to celebrate their triumph, one thunderously welcomes them

entgegen. Friede auf Erden.	with cannons. Peace on Earth.
Darum hüpfet und springet für	This is why the earth leaps and
Freuden die Erde.[19]	jumps in joy.

The last movement of the *Easter Oratorio* does not feature the cannons from Müller's celebration of the victorious hero, but the trumpets and timpani in the final chorus of the oratorio allude to the martial sphere Müller evokes in his sermon.

Ascension Oratorio BWV 11

The next major feast day in the liturgical year after Easter is Ascension Day, celebrated on a Thursday, thirty-nine days after Easter Sunday. The two major themes of Bach's composition for that day in 1735, the relationship between seeing and understanding and the presence of Christ in the heart (or soul) of the believer, connect it with the two other oratorios. The formal structure of the *Ascension Oratorio* resembles that of the *Christmas Oratorio* or Bach's passions: the biblical narrative is divided into several sections, each one followed by interpretations and meditations in recitatives, arias, and chorales. As in the *Christmas Oratorio*, the biblical recitatives are secco recitatives, only accompanied by the bass instruments, while the interpretative recitatives are accompanied by other instruments as well. Bach treats the story in four sections: Christ's farewell to his disciples (no. 2), his ascension (no. 5), the announcement of Christ's return (no. 7a), and the return of the disciples to Jerusalem (no. 7c). The movements are framed by two large-scale choral movements—the opening chorus "Lobet Gott in seinen Reichen" (Laud God in his kingdoms) and the final chorale setting "Wenn soll es doch geschehen" (When, do pray, shall it take place)—both featuring a massive instrumentation with trumpets, timpani, flutes, oboes, and strings.

Like the *Christmas Oratorio*, the oratorio for Ascension Day is based on parody movements borrowed from several earlier compositions (see Table 2 in Appendix B). In this case, Bach uses as a model a cantata for the inauguration of a renovation of the Thomas School in Leipzig, *Froher Tag, verlangte Stunden* BWV Anh. I, 18 and the Serenata *Auf, süß entzückende Gewalt* BWV Anh. I, 196. Both cantatas are lost, but it is possible to reconstruct them partly based on the texts that have come down to us and the music in the oratorio.

The first gospel recitative that follows the opening chorus describes how Jesus blessed his disciples and departed from them. The event is contemplated in the bass recitative that follows. The singer, accompanied by the two flutes, bemoans the departure of Jesus and describes the hot tears that are running down his cheeks. Bach depicts the flowing of the tears in little flute flourishes that appear between the lines of the text. The soft notes of the flutes, played staccato, in a short, detached style, almost let us see the individual tear drops (example 6.4).

The alto aria "Bleibe doch" asks Jesus to stay, since his absence was the reason for suffering. The aria has a mournful, sad feel. It would be wrong to see it only as a reflection of the departure of Jesus in the biblical narrative. It rather is the general desire of the soul for the presence of Jesus. As is typical of arias that are about the longing of the human soul for divine presence, Bach gives the part to the alto, here paired with the violin. The movement has an interesting history. It was originally composed for the Serenata *Auf, süß entzückenden Gewalt*. But Bach would later re-use the music for the *Agnus Dei* of his *B Minor Mass*, which was completed in the late 1740s.

Example 6.4: Bach, *Ascension Oratorio* BWV 11/3, mm. 1–6

The parody was possible because the texts, while expressing different theological ideas, do share the same affect of somber longing: in one case the longing for the presence of Jesus and in the other case the longing for Christ's mercy.

After the following recitative has reported that Christ had ascended into heaven and was sitting at the right hand of his father, the simple four-part chorale stanza confirms that God's son was now above everything else, even the angels and worldly rulers. Chorale stanzas in Bach's oratorios and passions often represent the perspective of the church or the Christian congregation. Thus, the text here shows that the church as a whole has understood the significance of Christ's ascension. The individual, however, might have a harder time comprehending what has just come to pass. The gospel recitative no. 7a describes how the disciples' eyes follow Jesus up to heaven. A little ascending line in the accompaniment (measure 2) traces their gazes up to the skies. They see but they do not comprehend. Just as the disciples in the *Easter Oratorio* had needed divine intervention to correctly interpret the empty grave and the shroud, two "men in white cloths" appear and sing "Ihr Männer von Galiläa, was stehet ihr und sehet gen Himmel?" (You men of Galilee, why are you standing and looking upto heaven?). They promise that the Ascension was not the end but that Christ will return. Bach sets the text first in simple, homophonic declamation and then continues with a canon between the two singers; one voice starts and the next one follows a beat later, with the same music a fifth lower. Bach scholar Hans-Joachim Schulze has convincingly suggested that this canon symbolized the two men (or angels) being in complete agreement, their message thus irrefutable.[20] Heinrich Müller suggests something similar in his interpretation of the two angels in the Resurrection narrative:

Dieser Engel waren zweene, und zweene, machen einen Band. Die Engel sind enträchtge Geister, verbunden zu dem einen, der ihrer aller Schöpffer ist, alle als einer in dem einen HErrn, dem sie alle dienen.[21]	The angels were two [in number] and two make a group. The angels are one in spirit, [they are] connected with the one who is the creator of all; they are all one in the one Lord they are serving.

The alto recitative "Ach ja, so komme bald zurück" (Ah yes! So come back soon, no. 7b) reiterates the longing for Christ's presence, thematically harkening back to the alto aria no. 4.

Only after the intervention of the angels do the men understand and return joyfully to Jerusalem (no. 7c).

The soprano aria "Jesu, deine Gnadenblicke" (Jesus, your gracious gazes I can see, no. 8) adds an important perspective to the story of Ascension Day. In the biblical narrative it is the hope for Christ's return that instills joy in the disciples, which eventually motivates them to embark on their journey back to Jerusalem. For Lutheran Christians in the seventeenth and early eighteenth centuries, however, the return of Christ was only the final step in three layers of divine presence: his presence in the past, in the future, and most significantly, his current presence in every single believer. Theologians in Bach's time explain that Jesus engages in a close relationship with the believer in the human heart. Inspired by the biblical *Song of Songs*, this presence of Christ is a mystical union (*unio mystica*) that is described by the image of the bride and bridegroom. In other words, it is a love relationship. I have already quoted the description of this mystical union by the seventeenth-century theologian Johann Arndt in Chapter Three, but it is so essential for theology and devotion around 1700 that I want to quote it again:

> The unification of the Lord Christ with the faithful soul is caused by the spiritual marriage and wedding. When the bridegroom arrives, the holy soul (*Seele*) is happy and pays exact and diligent attention to his presence; as his joyful, heart-refreshing and holy arrival drives away darkness and night. The heart has sweet joy, the waters of devotion flow, the soul melts for love, the spirit is full of joy, the affects and desires turn fervent, the love is ignited, the soul (*Gemüt*) rejoices, the mouth praises and extols and utters vows, and all the powers of the soul (*Seele*) rejoice in and because of the bridegroom. She (the soul) is full of joy, so I say, because she

has found the one who loves her and because he has taken her as a bride. She honors him. O what love! O what burning desire! O what conversations full of love! O what a chaste kiss, when the Holy Spirit descends, when the consoler overshadows, when the highest illuminates, when the word of the father is there, when (it) talks truth and when love embraces her warmly.[22]

As love constitutes divine presence, even after the Ascension of Christ, the soprano aria (no. 8) in the *Ascension Oratorio* reads:

Deine Liebe bleibt zurücke,	Your love remains behind,
Daß ich mich hier in der Zeit	So that I in the meantime, here
An der künftgen Herrlichkeit	In advance, already
Schon voraus im Geist erquicke,	Restore myself in my spirit by the future glory,
Wenn wir einst dort vor dir stehn.	When we one day stand before you, there.

This romantic relationship, however, is constituted by Jesus himself, as the first two lines of the aria point out:

Jesu, deine Gnadenblicke	Jesus, your gracious gazes I can see
Kann ich doch beständig sehn.	Steadfastly indeed.

The unusual term "Gnadenblick" (gracious gaze) appears occasionally in the theological and devotional literature from the seventeenth and eighteenth centuries and denotes the merciful attention of God or Christ towards man. More generally, "Gnadenblick" could also be used for secular rulers who regarded their subjects mercifully. In other words, the term describes a power relationship between the subject and the object of the gaze. At the same time, it connotes merciful

benevolence on the part of the one looking. The efficacy of
Christ's merciful gaze is similarly important for the understanding of "Gnadenblick." Heinrich Müller, in a sermon for
the sixteenth Sunday after Trinity, interprets the encounter
between Jesus and the widow from Nain, who hopes that Jesus
might revive her dead son (Luke 7:12–13). She does not dare
look at Jesus, yet he sees her:

Aber wiewohl sie den HErrn nicht sahe, sahe er sie doch. Auch dann blickt dich JEsus gnädig an, wann du ihn mit grosser Angst mit seiner Hülffe nicht erblicken kanst. Ob du mit den blöden Glaubens-Augen durch die Creutz-Wolcken nicht hindurch dringen kanst, so dringt er doch zu dir hindurch mit seinem hellen Gnaden-Auge.[23]	Even though she did not see the Lord, he did see her. Jesus looks even then at you mercifully when you, in great fear, cannot see his assistance. If you cannot look through the cross-clouds with your fearful [shy] faith-eyes, his gaze will reach you with his bright mercy-eye.

The divine gaze is efficacious; and it is an expression of divine
love. We have seen repeatedly, both in the discussion of the
Magnificat and of the *Christmas Oratorio*, that divine mercy
and divine love are interrelated concepts. Bach frequently sets
texts about God's mercy as love duets. The present aria is not
a love duet but it draws a similar connection by relating the
"Gnadenblicke" in line 1 of the text to Jesus' love in line 3.
Again, divine love and mercy are thought of as one.

The soprano aria is also about "seeing." Seeing and understanding are here resolved: the believer can see the
"Gnadenblicke," the gazes of mercy. The human gaze is concep-
tualized as a response to the divine gaze. It is not the gaze of
enlightened empiricism, but a visual (and intellectual) perception that is divinely mediated. This harkens back to an earlier

moment in the narrative, when the disciples depended on the two angels to understand what they were seeing (and where to look in the first place). Heinrich Müller, in one of his Ascension Day sermons, similarly elaborates on the inability of men to understand and the necessity of divine revelation. Here, the guiding light is not the encounter with heavenly creatures, as in the narrative, but with the divine revelation through the Word of God and described as well with a visual metaphor as the "light on the path" (Psalm 119:105):

Bey den Jüngern war der Unglaube und des Hertzens Härtigkeit. Sie waren nicht nur ungläubig, sondern auch halsstarrig, haben nicht allein an der Auferstehung des HERRN gezweiffelt, sondern auch zweiffels ohn denen, die sie verkündiget, widersprochen . . . So hindert offt die falsche Meynung den wahren Glauben, so verhärtet sie das Hertz, daß es der Wahrheit nicht nur nicht zustimmt, sondern auch widerspricht. Darum entschlage dich alles eitlen Dünckels, und prüfe in allen Dingen, welches sey des HERRN Wille. Der Probierstein ist GOttes Wort. Das soll dir seyn ein Licht auf allen deinen Wegen.[24]

The disciples had disbelief and hardness of the heart. Not only did they lack faith but they were stubborn as well; not only did they doubt the resurrection of the Lord surely, but they also contradicted the ones who announced the resurrection . . . Thus, often wrong beliefs impede on the true faith; [wrong beliefs] harden the heart so that it not only cannot agree with the truth [any more] but even contradicts [the truth]. Therefore, write off all your vain arrogance and search in all things for the will of the Lord. The touchstone is God's word. It shall be for you a light on all your paths.

Bach's setting of the soprano aria in the *Ascension Oratorio* is particularly intriguing. The aria has a so-called bassetto texture. That means that the deep bass voice is missing; instead violins and viola play a high supporting voice. Additionally, Bach introduces the two flutes and the oboe as solo instruments that accompany the soprano. The texture gives the aria a very delicate sound. But the "high" sound also alludes to the fact that Jesus is now on high, that he has ascended to heaven.

The final chorale setting broadens the perspective again and implores Jesus to return in glory: "Komm, stelle dich doch ein!" (Come [o day], pray do appear!). The music, with its prominent trumpet parts, not only looks back to the opening movement but it also resembles the final chorale setting of the *Christmas Oratorio*, which Bach had performed only four and a half months earlier. The lines from the chorale are combined with a large-scale instrumental accompaniment, which features a polychoral dialogue between the different instrumental groups, creating the impression of an instrumental concerto. The *Ascension Oratorio* implores Christ to return so that his faithful can greet and kiss him. Then they will see him as he is. Until then "an Inquiry into the understanding" might be "pleasant and useful," as Locke had stated, but human perception remains imperfect.

CHAPTER SEVEN

BETWEEN OPERA AND ARCHITECTURE

THE *B MINOR MASS* BWV 232

Crucifixus etiam pro nobis (BWV 232[II]/5)

In early 2011, the *New York Times* music critic Anthony Tommasini published a series of articles with a ranking of the ten greatest composers of classical music.[1] It is no surprise that the leader of the ranking was none other than Johann Sebastian Bach. One can raise the question of whether such a ranking is useful, or even possible, considering that Tommasini was comparing composers over a span of some 300 years. Even the critic himself admits this. But let us stay with it for a moment and take the idea one step further. If Bach is indeed the best composer, what is his best work? What would be in Bach's top ten? The *St Matthew Passion* would probably be up there. Other pieces in Bach's top ten would most likely be his *Musical Offering*, the *Art of Fugue*, his *Brandenburg Concertos*, and everybody has probably one or two other pieces they would want to add to the list. And which work by Bach would take the prize for the best? Again, the question seems futile, but if we ask nineteenth-century conductor and composer Hans Georg Nägeli (1773–1836), the answer is clear. In an advertisement from 1818, he labeled Johann Sebastian Bach's

B Minor Mass the "greatest artwork of all times and all people."[2] This evaluation is not so far off Tommasini's ranking. If Bach is the greatest composer, the *B Minor Mass* would be his greatest work.

Advertising Greatness

Nägeli had bought the original manuscript of the *B Minor Mass* from Carl Philipp Emanuel Bach's heir and intended to publish the first edition of the piece.[3] But he was not successful. It took until 1832, when the German publisher Simrock printed a piano reduction of the mass. In 1833, the first half of the score was published by Nägeli. He announced that the second half would appear in print in 1834, but when he died two years later the piece had not yet been printed. In 1845, finally, the whole score was published.[4]

Two other editors in the nineteenth century also failed to publish the mass, or parts thereof. In 1816, the English composer Samuel Wesley (1766–1837), one of the forerunners in the rediscovery of Bach in the British Isles,[5] made an attempt to publish the *Credo* of the mass, but was not successful. The article from 1821—which I have quoted in the introduction to this book, speculating about what Bach's oratorios might have looked like—gives a sense of the difficult reception Bach's vocal music was still facing in the early years of the nineteenth century. Similarly, in 1818, only one month later than Nägeli, Georg Johann Daniel Poelchau (1773–1836), a member of the Berlin Singakademie and an important collector of Bach's manuscripts, considered printing the score of the mass—a plan that was never put into effect.[6]

In 1818, the *B Minor Mass* had still never been performed in its entirety; only composers and music historians were interested in Bach's works. Although his music was never completely forgotten, he was a composer for specialists but his works were rarely performed in a concert setting.[7] The few pieces by Bach which were published during the first third of the nineteenth century served primarily as examples for composition, as études for performers, or were understood as monuments of music history,[8] but they were not intended to be played in public.[9] Bach's music was considered music for the eye and the brain—not for the ear. This would change when Felix Mendelssohn Bartholdy (1809–1847) performed Bach's *St Matthew Passion* in Berlin in 1829, and introduced Bach to the concert hall.[10] But even then it was a long time before Bach's large-scale works were considered an integral part of the concert repertoire. Although several movements had been performed during the first half of the century, the first complete public performance of the *B Minor Mass* occurred after 1859.[11]

What would have been Johann Sebastian Bach's response to this discussion about his greatness? He probably would not have called himself the greatest composer ever; however, contemporary sources do suggest that he held his *B Minor Mass* in very high esteem—which is reflected in his intensive work on this particular piece for over fifteen years. In fact, Nägeli's unsuccessful campaign was not the first time that the *B Minor Mass* had been subject to advertising. The history of the mass started as a sort of advertising campaign. Bach himself created the first parts of the mass, the *Kyrie* and *Gloria*, in order to apply for the title of court composer in Dresden in 1733. To understand this, we have to go back to the early 1730s, when Bach was cantor at St Thomas in Leipzig.

Bach was deeply dissatisfied with his position at St Thomas, which he had held at this point for close to a decade. In a letter to his friend Georg Erdmann in 1730,[12] Bach lamented his situation in Leipzig and asked whether his friend could find him a decent position elsewhere. We do not have Erdmann's reply, but the attempt was obviously not successful. In the following years, Bach tried to convince the court of the Elector of Saxony in Dresden to award him the prestigious title of "court composer." To that end, between 1732 and 1735 he composed at least eight secular cantatas in honor of the court in the Saxon capital. Most of the cantatas, the *drammi per musica* I discussed in Chapter Three, resemble little operatic scenes and use dialogues and allegorical or mythical characters. Dresden was at this time a center for opera performances in Germany.

History played into Bach's hand as well. In 1733, the old Elector of Saxony, Friedrich August I (The Strong, 1670–1733), had died and his son, Friedrich August II (1696–1763), had just been inaugurated into his new position. Bach offered his services to the new ruler and sent him the following letter:

To Your Royal Highness I submit in deepest devotion the present small work of that science which I have achieved in *musique*, with the most wholly submissive prayer that Your Highness will look upon it with Most Gracious Eyes, according to Your Highness's World-Famous Clemency and not according to the poor *composition*; and thus deign to take me under Your Most Mighty Protection. For some years and up to the present moment, I have had the *Directorium* of the Music in the two principal churches in Leipzig, but innocently had to suffer one injury or another, and on occasion also a diminution of the fees accruing to me in this office; but these injuries would disappear altogether if Your Royal Highness would grant me the favor of conferring upon me a title of Your Highness's Court Capelle, and would let Your High Command for the issuing of such a document go forth to the proper place. Such a most gracious fulfillment of my most humble prayer will bind me to unending devotion, and I offer myself in most indebted obedience to show at all times, upon Your Royal Highness's Most Gracious Desire, my untiring zeal in the composition of music for the church as well as for the orchestra, and to devote my entire forces to the service of Your Highness, remaining in unceasing fidelity Your Royal Highness's most humble and most obedient servant.

Dressden, July 27, 1733   JOHANN SEBASTIAN BACH[13]

The music, the "small work of science," that Bach mentions in the letter, was the beginning of the very piece that Nägeli would later call "the greatest artwork," the *Kyrie* and the *Gloria* of the *B Minor Mass*. It would take until 1736 for Bach to receive the title of court composer in Dresden; however, he eventually succeeded.

The music he sent to the court in 1733 was not entirely new. In fact, most of the movements were borrowed from earlier works composed by Bach in the previous twenty years for various occasions (see Table 3 in Appendix B). The practice of recycling older musical material and providing it with a new text is called a parody. Parody was a familiar technique in seventeenth- and eighteenth-century music, and was similarly employed by most of Bach's contemporaries. Two of Bach's masterworks are based on parodies, the *Christmas Oratorio* and the *B Minor Mass*. The way Bach creates his parodies, however, is significantly different in the two works. In the *Christmas Oratorio*, written in 1734, Bach parodied recently composed secular pieces and the texts were conceived especially for these pre-existing movements. Therefore, Bach could use the music without major changes. This was different in the *B Minor Mass*. The text for the mass was part of the traditional Christian liturgy and had its roots in the Middle Ages. It was not possible to adapt the words to fit the music. Bach, therefore, had to rework the older movements more thoroughly. In some cases, these revisions are rather significant and occasionally Bach only employs sections of the original movements.

The pieces Bach chose for the mass are some of the best and most demanding works he had composed. The "small work of science" that Bach sent to Dresden is really his "best of." The selection of pieces reflected his accomplishment as a composer at this point in his career. Maybe this was not the "greatest artwork of all times and all people," but it stood as a sample of the best Bach had to offer as a composer of sacred music. But Bach did more than just present some of his most intriguing pieces. He was aware of the style of mass composition that was popular in Dresden at this time and he shaped the pieces to fit that prevalent style. He used, for instance, a five-part choir, which is unusual in his own compositions, but common in Dresden masses. He also included several movements in the old *stile antico*, a polyphonic style that was rooted in the music of the sixteenth century and was similarly popular in some of the masses at the court in Dresden. And, finally, the division of the mass into several independent movements ('cantata mass') conformed to Dresden models as well.

Love Duets

Dresden was also famous as a center of Italian opera in Germany. We would not expect operatic music in a liturgical setting; however, we do find traces of contemporary dramatic music here. What are most operas about? Love! Almost no opera is without a love story: Orpheus and Euridice; Papageno and Papagena; Lohengrin and Elsa; Porgy and Bess. What is the main subject of the mass? It is the text of the Christian liturgy, the cry *Kyrie eleison*–Lord, have mercy; the praise of God in the *Gloria in excelsis*; the confession of faith in the Creed, *Credo in unum Deum*, and the celebration of the Eucharistic mystery in the *Sanctus* and *Agnus Dei*. The five parts of the mass are the backbone for the Christian liturgies, both in the Lutheran tradition, in which Bach lived, and in the Catholic tradition at the Dresden court.

For a Lutheran Christian of the eighteenth century, the mass was also (and foremost) a celebration of love: the love of God and the love between Christ and the believer. Contemporary theology and religious poetry described the relationship between Christ and the faithful as an almost intimate relationship, borrowing the imagery from the biblical *Song of Songs*: the bride and the bridegroom. We have seen this imagery repeatedly in Bach's major vocal works, from the early *Magnificat* to the oratorios from the 1730s. The bridal imagery of the *unio mystica* was a major influence on the texts Bach set. One of the most famous pieces in this tradition is the cantata *Wachet auf, ruft uns die Stimme* BWV 140 (from 1731). Based on motives from the *Song of Songs*, the librettist wrote the following duet:

Soprano	Bass
My beloved is mine!	And I am yours!
Nothing shall separate our love!	
I will join thee	—you shall join me—
To wander through Heaven's roses,	
There shall be the fullness of joy and gladness.	

It would be easy to imagine this conversation in a baroque opera—but love here becomes the key metaphor to describe the relationship between God and humanity. Contemporary opera had developed stereotypes for love duets: "parallel thirds and sixths, diatonic melodic lines, a *galant* mixture of duple and triple figures, straightforward harmonies, expressive appoggiaturas, and weak-beat phrase endings that resolve downward as 'sighs'."[14] In plain words: simple, yet expressive melodies, sung by two voices in mostly parallel motion. The two voices move in the same direction, which signifies harmony on a musical and interpersonal level, and the parallel thirds are also extremely harmonious intervals: the sonic equivalent of love. We have discussed several movements of this type in earlier chapters, such as the *Et misericordia* from the *Magnificat* BWV 243 and "Herr, dein Mitleid" from the *Christmas Oratorio* BWV 248.

We find no fewer than three movements that follow the model of the "love duet" in the *B Minor mass*. Two of these moments appear in the first two parts of the mass, the *Kyrie* and the *Gloria*, which Bach had composed for the opera-loving court in Dresden. In addition, later in his career, Bach added one other duet in the *Credo*, the confession of faith. All three of these duets exhibit the stylistic characteristics I mentioned earlier: two voices moving in loving harmony and an expressive voice leading. The first example is the *Christe* from the first section of the mass, the *Kyrie* (example 7.1). Bach's musical realization of the Christological text has to be understood within the emotional Jesus piety we have explored in earlier chapters. As theologians such as Heinrich Müller and Johann Arndt had emphasized, the relationship between Christ and the believer was understood as a love relationship. This relationship found its musical equivalent in the love duet that

Example 7.1: Bach, *B Minor Mass* BWV 232¹/2, mm. 10–13

composers like Bach borrowed from contemporary opera. This must not be misunderstood as a dramatic personification—Jesus as the first soprano, the believer as the second one. Rather, it is the idea of love in general that is represented in this movement.

The other two duets in the *B Minor Mass* have a similar function. The second one is the duet *Domine Deus* from the *Gloria*. With its many parallel thirds and sixths, the movement similarly exhibits the typical features of a "love duet." And like the *Christe*, it references Christ directly—*Domine Deus, Agnus Dei, Filius Patris* (Lord God, Lamb of God, Son of the Father). The third love duet finally occurs in the *Credo* section. After two massive movements praising God the Father, the third movement honors Christ: *Et unum dominum, Jesum Christum* (And one Lord, Jesus Christ). One could have expected a majestic movement, as the words are addressed to the *Lord* Jesus Christ. But within the context of eighteenth-century devotion, it is understandable that Bach decided to emphasize the personal relationship between Christ and the believer (who confesses his or her faith) by composing another love duet. Again, it is not a dramatic staging of love, but rather a sonic representation of this love.

I have highlighted the love duet because it helps us understand how intrinsically intertwined are the secular, theological, and personal aspects that shape a piece as complex and multilayered as the *B Minor Mass*. A second feature that bridges the sacred and the secular is the structure, which reflects ideals of balance and proportion in contemporary architecture.

Architecture

Music and architecture of the baroque period participate in similar paradigms. One of the basic principles of architecture around 1700 is the symmetric ground plan. The palace of Versailles, France, built by the "Sun-King" Louis XIV, is the paradigmatic example of this esthetic and it would become the model for numerous other palaces in subsequent decades (figure 7.1). The centerpiece was the main building, which itself is axial-symmetric. It is framed by two huge, majestic side-wings. Norbert Elias has pointed out in his influential study *The Court Society*[15] the extent to which the architecture of Versailles reflected (and shaped) society and how the European nobility, by imitating the architecture of the palace, also adopted the social paradigms of the French absolutist court.[16] Thus, the palace served not only as an architectural

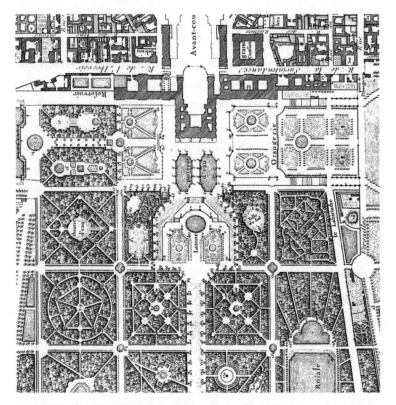

Figure 7.1: Versailles, plan by Jean Delagrive (public domain)

paradigm, but also as an emanation of the sociological structure of the late seventeenth and early eighteenth centuries. In
Germany, several residences were built (or re-built) according
to this model—although on a much smaller scale. But the
symmetric outline was nevertheless preserved. Bach was surely
familiar with this type of architecture, as the palace
Friedrichswerth in Gotha (close to Weimar) was constructed
around 1710, based on the same principle.[17]

Balanced proportion and symmetry, which are the underlying principles of Versailles, were seen in a baroque worldview
as signs of perfection, mirroring the beauty and perfection of

divine creation. An earlier example of this concept of perfection is the title page of Michael Praetorius's music print *Musae Sioniae* (1605), one of the most successful musical collections in the seventeenth century (figure 7.2). God the Father is depicted in the upper register of the picture, symbolized by the divine name in Hebrew letters; beneath him is the lamb, Jesus Christ. God is framed by the evangelists (two on either side), and he and Christ are surrounded by the heavenly choirs. The image combines cosmology with "musicology." Music-making on earth is but a reflection of this heavenly scenario: two choirs sing on either side of a balcony, framing the great organ in the middle. Even in music-making, the symmetry on earth mirrors the heavenly symmetrical perfection.[18] The purpose of art at this time—be it architecture, visual arts, or music—was to reflect this divine perfection and to praise God in this way. We can find a similar symmetrical outline in numerous pieces by Johann Sebastian Bach, but only in a few cases is this outline as consequential (and as theologically significant) as it is in the *B Minor Mass*.

Kyrie

The first part of the mass, the *Kyrie*, is constructed on these principles. The middle section, the *Christe eleison* (Christ, have mercy), is framed by two huge movements for choir and orchestra, imploring God for mercy (*Kyrie eleison*—Lord, have mercy) through a polyphonic fabric. The first *Kyrie* is composed as a modern fugue with an instrumental theme and—at least at the beginning—independent instrumental voices. When the text *Kyrie eleison* is repeated after the *Christe eleison*, the texture is again polyphonic, but in a very different way. While the first *Kyrie* had an instrumental character, the second one is

Figure 7.2: Michael Praetorius, *Musae Sioniae* (1605), title page (public domain)

influenced by the polyphonic vocal style of the early modern period, known as *stile antico* (old style),[19] or "Palestrina style" after the famous Roman sixteenth-century composer, Giovanni Pierluigi da Palestrina (1525–1594). The instruments in the second *Kyrie* essentially follow the vocal parts. The whole piece could easily be performed without the instruments. There were several motivations for Bach to use this compositional technique. One reason is Bach's own interest in different musical styles and his aim to improve his own personal style during his own lifetime. He always looked for compositional challenges, and it was a challenge to compose a movement in this elaborate vocal style. The other motivation follows from the purpose of the mass as a "job application" for the court in Dresden: Bach was familiar with the musical preferences at the court in Dresden and he was aware that the *stile antico* was very frequently used by composers in the Saxon capital at this time. In other words, writing some movements of the mass in Palestrina style was, at least in part, an element of his advertising strategy.

Music example 7.2 shows the beginning of the second *Kyrie*. The bass begins with a long melodic idea, sharpened by chromaticisms (progressions in half-tone steps) and supported by the bassoon. The tenor enters with the same melody and is accompanied by the viola. The different timbre of the reed instrument and the string instrument makes the polyphonic fabric more transparent. The same applies when the alto (with the oboe) and the soprano (with oboe and flute) eventually enter. The instrumentation, characteristic of the German seventeenth-century ideal of *Spaltklang* (divided sounds), underscores the polyphonic texture of this setting.

Several other aspects of this mass point to models in the Saxon capital. One is the slow introduction, opening the whole

Example 7.2: Bach, *B Minor Mass* BWV 232¹/3, mm. 1-9

Example 7.3: *Kyrie* fugues by Wilderer and Bach

Kyrie section. We can find similar introductions in other masses in Dresden. There is one in particular, composed by Johann Hugo von Wilderer (1670/71–1724), which is so similar that it likely served as a model for Bach. Even the theme of the first fugue in Bach's mass is similar to Wilderer's *Kyrie* fugue (example 7.3).[20] Bach copied the mass by Wilderer around 1730, so we know for sure that he was familiar with the piece.[21] On the other hand, Bach did not just imitate the model but composed a much more complex setting. While Wilderer's introduction is a straightforward, homophonic piece, Bach's introduction starts with a dense homophonic texture as well, but the composer enriches the setting with syncopations and sharp chromaticisms.

Kyrie I and II represent the two side-wings of our "palace." The central section of the building, the *Christe eleison*, is composed in contrast. It is set for two voices and violins. The character is quite intimate and it is the first example of a love duet in the mass.[22] Within the architecture of the first section of the mass, the duet occupies the central position: the "main building" of the palace, framed by the two *Kyrie* side-wings.

Gloria

The second section of the *B Minor Mass*, the *Gloria*, consists of nine movements. Again, this section of the mass is framed by two huge movements for choir and orchestra which, in this case, are stylistically equivalent. Both are inspired by models of the eighteenth-century instrumental concerto.[23] The first movement of the *Gloria* even starts as an instrumental concerto with the orchestra, presenting the musical material before the voices develop this motivic material in a dense dialogue with the instruments. The jubilation of the angels is expressed by the use of trumpets and timpani. The last movement of the *Gloria*, the *Cum sancto spirito* (With the Holy Spirit), has the same character. Again a concerto, and again the sound is shaped by the use of trumpets and percussion. These two side-wings frame the rest of the *Gloria*, which, as we will see shortly, exhibits an outline that revolves around a central piece.

The second movement is the *Et in terra pax* (And peace on earth). Since the text focuses on men on earth, Bach empha-sizes the human element, the voice. While in the *Gloria in excelsis* the music had been dominated by the musical material presented and developed by the instruments in the long instru-mental introduction, now the voices start in a quiet four-part setting; the instruments join only one measure later, echoing the motivic material of the vocal choir.

After this juxtaposition of heavenly orchestra and earthly voices, Bach combines the solo soprano with an obbligato violin, in the virtuosic aria, *Laudamus te*. Some Bach scholars have argued that this movement was likewise composed to fit the taste of the court in Dresden, and that the composer might have had one soprano in particular in mind when he wrote the piece,[24] the Dresden prima donna Faustina Bordoni (1697–1781), wife of celebrated opera composer Johann Adolph Hasse. Indeed, what we know about her singing from Bach's contemporary, Johann Joachim Quantz (1697–1773), fits perfectly with the demands of this aria:

Her execution was articulate and brilliant. She had a fluent tongue for pronouncing words rapidly and distinctly, and a flexible throat for divisions, with so beautiful and quick a shake, that she could put it in motion upon short notice, just when she would. The passages might be smooth, or by leaps, or consist of iterations of the same tone—their execution was equally easy to her.[25]

In the following *Gratias agimus* Bach returns back to the Palestrina style of the Renaissance, which we have already heard in the second *Kyrie*. The vocalists are accompanied by the instruments, and Bach's aim is to reach the highest degree of transparency in the polyphonic texture by supporting every vocal voice with a different instrumental timbre (*Spaltklang*, divided sounds). Here, Bach re-uses a polyphonic movement from the cantata *Wir danken dir, Gott* BWV 29,[26] composed in 1731, and overlays it with the Latin text. Interestingly, Bach not only parodies an older movement that is similar in character to the new text,[27] but the old and the new texts express almost the same sentiment: *Gratias agimus tibi* and "Wir danken dir, Gott": both mean "we thank you."

Although no sources for a model composition exist, it is very likely that the music of the *Domine Deus* was taken from an earlier work as well; maybe from the now lost cantata *Ihr Häuser des Himmels* BWV 193a, from 1727.[28] It is a movement for a solo instrument (this time the flute), which begins with a concerto-like dialogue with the orchestra until soprano and tenor enter to engage in a dialogue with the instrumental soloist and the orchestra. The movement is the second of our love duets in the *B Minor Mass* and, like the *Christe eleison*, has a Christological focus. The instrumentation of this movement is theologically intriguing. One could expect that the text

Example 7.4: Bach, *B Minor Mass* BWV 232¹/8, mm. 1–3

Domine Deus, Rex coelestis, Deus Pater omnipotens (Lord God, heavenly King, God the omnipotent Father) would be set as a celebration of divine glory, with a scoring that involved the trumpets, timpani, and the whole choir. Instead, Bach opens the movement with a single flute, accompanied only by the basso continuo; and when the strings enter one measure later, they have to play *con sordino* (with the mute) (example 7.4).

The soft sound does not seem to fit the first part of the text for this movement. It does, however, reflect its end: *Domine Deus, Agnus Dei, Filius Patris* (Lord God, Lamb of God, Son of the Father). The musical expression of this whole movement is conceived from the *theologia crucis*, the theology of the cross, at the end of the text. Bach's compositional decision is probably influenced by Luther's *theologia crucis*. Martin Luther wrote in 1518, in his *Heidelberg Disputation*:

He deserves to be called a theologian, however, who comprehends the visible and manifest things of God seen through suffering and the cross ... Now it is not sufficient for anyone, and it does him no good to recognize God in his glory and majesty, unless he recognizes him in the humility and shame of the cross ... A theologian of glory

calls evil good and good evil. A theologian of the cross calls
the thing what it actually is.[29]

According to Luther, God can only be understood if he is seen
as being revealed in the crucified Jesus Christ. In other words,
the *Deus Pater omnipotens* (God the omnipotent Father) had to
be understood from the vantage point of the *Domine Deus,
Agnus Dei* (Lord God, Lamb of God). While it was the *theologia crucis* that influenced the overall somber character of the
movement, the use of the love duet was motivated by a more
recent development in the theology of the passion in Lutheran
Germany, which highlighted even more the understanding of
the passion of Christ as an expression of divine affection.[30] The
German theologian Heinrich Müller, one of the most influential preachers at this time, wrote in a sermon, published in
1679:

> The Apostle Paul admonishes his Timothy that he always
> should bear in his mind Jesus, the crucified ... We recog-
> nize his love by the fact that he gave his life for us, when
> we were still his enemies. Thus it is proper that we repay
> his love with love. But it is the character of love that she
> always keeps in mind what she loves. When she goes or
> stands, she sees the beloved in her thoughts. We, who love
> the Lord Jesus, should always keep him in mind. The
> crucified Jesus is the only true comfort for our souls.[31]

As I pointed out in the analysis of the *St Matthew Passion* in
Chapter Five, Bach's contemporaries understood the cross to
be a sign for God's love towards mankind. The appropriate
human reaction was to answer this love with love. Bach's
choice of an intimate duet for the text of this movement of the

mass directly reflects this understanding of the cross. And again, theology correlates with architecture, as the *Domine Deus* is the centerpiece of the *Gloria* of the *B Minor Mass*.

The following *Qui tollis*, based on a movement from the 1723 cantata *Schauet doch und sehet* BWV 46, is a gloomy, harmonically rich chorus expressing the suffering and death of Jesus Christ. The original text in the cantata has a similar grieving character. Thus, it was easy for Bach to adjust the music to the new text.[32] The words in BWV 46 were taken from the Lamentations of Jeremiah 1:12: "Behold and see if there be any sorrow like unto my sorrow, which is done unto me, herewith the Lord hath afflicted me in the day of his fierce anger."

Some of the musical ideas in the chorus might remind a listener of the end of Bach's *St John Passion*. Both movements speak about the suffering and dying of Jesus and the meaning of his death for humanity. The cantata movement was composed only eight months before the passion and Bach employs a similar musical language for both. Through the parody in the mass, we now have an intriguing connection between the end of the passion and the invocation of the suffering Lamb of God in the *Gloria*.

The *Qui tollis* is followed by an intimate alto aria on the text *Qui sedes ad dexteram Patris* (You who sit at the right hand of the Father). The alto is accompanied by oboe d'amore solo and strings. Most of the masses from the repertoire used at the Dresden court (and Bach's own *Kyrie-Gloria* masses BWV 233–236), the *Qui sedes* and the *Qui tollis* in one movement.[33] Here in the *B Minor Mass*, however, Bach divides the text into two pieces, which allows him to give each of them their appropriate treatment. While the *Qui tollis* is mournful in tone, the *Qui sedes* has a dance-like character, celebrating the elevated Christ. It was the Bach biographer Philipp Spitta

(1841–1894) who in the 1870s interpreted this as a result of theological reflection:

> Here his theological learning … stood him in good stead. Doctrinal theology assigns to Christ a threefold office—as Prophet, High Priest, and King. The text offered no opening for treating the prophetic aspect—only the priestly and kingly. As, in considering Christ as a priest, there is again a distinction between Atonement and Mediation (*munus satis-factionis* and *intercessionis*), Bach has figured the former by the chorus *Qui tollis*, and the latter by the alto aria *Qui sedes*, but in close connection, for the key is the same in both.[34]

It is doubtful that the dogma of the threefold office formed the background for these two movements, since one of the offices is missing and there is no real evidence that Bach wanted to allude to this theological concept. However, Spitta correctly senses a theological motivation for the relationship between the two movements. Instead of the threefold office of Christ, the binary opposition of the characters of the two movements supports a different thesis, that Bach emphasizes the difference between the human nature of Christ (visible in his suffering) and the divine nature, expressed by his ascension and his sitting at the right-hand of God, the Father. This aspect is of crucial importance in Martin Luther's theology. In his explanation of the second article of the Creed in his *Small Catechism*, the reformer stated:

> I believe that Jesus Christ, true God, begotten of the Father from eternity, and also true man, born of the virgin Mary, is my Lord, who has redeemed me, a lost and condemned creature, delivered me and freed me from all sins, from death, and from the power of the devil, not with silver and

gold but with his holy and precious blood and with his
innocent sufferings and death, in order that I may be his,
live under him in his kingdom, and serve him in everlasting
righteousness, innocence, and blessedness, even as he is
risen from the dead and lives and reigns to all eternity.[35]

Just as the *theologia crucis* is central to Luther's theological
thinking, the double nature of Christ as both human and
divine is, for Luther (and the Lutheran tradition), an inevi-
table precondition for salvation. It seems likely that Bach
wanted to reflect this duality in his music.

The *Gloria*'s second-to-last movement is the *Quoniam tu
solus sanctus* (For only you are holy), sung by the bass and
accompanied by corno da caccia and two bassoons. This
unusual combination of instruments gives the movement a
very solemn character that is appropriate for the invocation of
divine sanctity. The corno da caccia, considered a royal instrument, symbolizes the nobility of Christ the King. The *Gloria*
ends with a concerto-grosso-like movement, *Cum Sancto
Spiritu* (With the Holy Spirit), performed by the choir and
the full orchestra: with trumpets, timpani, flutes, oboes, strings,
bassoon, and basso continuo. Bach returns to the musical
forces of the first movement of the *Gloria*. The celebratory
fanfares in the trumpets and the choruses at the beginning and
the end of the *Gloria* balance each other perfectly. The architecture of this "building" is again symmetrical, a musical palace
for the glory of God. Framed by the concerto-like side-wings,
and the other movements praising God, the central section
speaks about the believer's relationship with God, which is—
in concord with contemporary theology—a relationship of
deepest love, rooted in Christ's suffering; and this love is
expressed by the love duet.

With the *Cum Sancto Spiritu*, the mass Bach composed for the court in Dresden in 1733 ends. We do not know whether or not these pieces were ever performed in Dresden or in Leipzig. The sources Bach sent to Dresden do not show any signs of a performance, and it was nearly fifteen years until Bach began to complete his mass cycle. When he returned to work on the mass in the late 1740s, he again parodied several older cantata movements and set them to the Latin texts of the mass. He again picked some of his most remarkable pieces, continuing the concept of the first two parts of the mass as a "best of" and a reflection of his accomplishments as a composer. But now the goal was different. While the *Kyrie* and *Gloria* served as part of his application for the title of "court composer" at the electoral court in Dresden, the completion of the mass had no external motivations that we know of. Rather, it was part of the encyclopedic series of works Bach created towards the end of his life, which represented different aspects of his style: the *Art of Fugue* is his treatise on counterpoint while the *B Minor Mass* would become the crowning example of his vocal style.

Credo

The introductory movement of the *Credo*, a polyphonic piece, was according to recent research composed about 1747/8 and might have served as a slow introduction to a Creed by another composer.[36] But only a short time later Bach began to complete his mass and integrated this movement into his own *Credo*. The following *Patrem omnipotentem* (Father omnipotent) is a parody of a movement composed around 1729 (*Gott, wie dein Name, so ist auch dein Ruhm* BWV 171). Like the earlier example of the *Gratias agimus* from the *Gloria*, the text of the model composition was already very close to the Latin parody.

Both texts express the power and might of God the Father and therefore have a similar effect.

The two opening movements of the *Credo*, while both composed for choir, represent two different musical styles, the *stile antico* (Palestrina style) in the introduction and the modern, concerto-like texture in the *Patrem omnipotentem*. But Bach not only juxtaposes an old and a new style, he also juxtaposes old and new musical material. The first movement of the *Credo* uses an old Gregorian chant, a melody that was still used in the liturgy in Leipzig during Bach's time (example 7.5).

Bach again establishes a symmetrical balance between the beginning and the end of the *Credo* by returning to the same types of movement for the penultimate and last movements of the Creed. The penultimate movement is a piece in old Palestrina style with the text *Confiteor unum baptisma* (I confess the one baptism) while the *Credo* ends with the modern, concerto-like *Et expecto resurrectionem mortuorum* (And I await the resurrection of the dead). The *Confiteor* again quotes material from the old chant Bach had already used in the opening movement. In the *Confiteor*, however, the melody is hidden in the lower voices and treated as a canon.[37] The connection between the beginning and end of the *Credo* not only creates a sense of symmetry and balance, it also highlights the thematic correspondence between the opening lines of the Creed and its end. Bach composed both movements in *stile antico* and both express a human reaction to the divine mystery. to believe and to confess. *Credo*—I believe ... *Confiteor*—I confess.

The two massive side-wings of the *Credo*-palace frame seven individual movements. Similar to the architecture of *Kyrie* and *Gloria*, the setting of the Creed has a centerpiece as well, which highlights a central theological idea. However, in

Example 7.5: Bach, *B Minor Mass* BWV 232^{II}/1, mm. 1–8

this case it is not a Christological love duet but the movement that expresses the love between God and humanity in the most poignant way, the *Crucifixus etiam pro nobis* (Crucified also for us). As we have seen earlier, the *theologia crucis* was a corner stone in Lutheran theology and seventeenth-century theologians like Heinrich Müller expanded this theology of the cross into a theology of divine love and affection.

The genesis of the *Credo* highlights how important this aspect was for the composer. Bach had originally only composed eight movements. The text *Et incarnatus est* (And was incarnate) was simply included in the previous movement, *Et in unum Dominum* (And [I believe] in the one Lord). When he reworked the piece, he inserted a separate movement for the *Et incarnatus est*, to make sure that the *Crucifixus* indeed formed the middle of the whole *Credo*.

The *Crucifixus* is the oldest movement in the entire mass. Bach composed it in 1714 in Weimar for the cantata *Weinen, Klagen, Sorgen, Zagen* BWV 12 and reworked it for his mass. Some scholars have identified the repeated quarter notes in the bass of the *Crucifixus* with the hammering of the nails and the flutes with the drops of Christ's blood. But even without a metaphorical interpretation, the movement—with its chromatic voice leading, dissonant harmonies, and a sigh-motive at the end of the word *"crucifixus"*—reflects these texts and depicts the death and suffering of Jesus Christ in a moving way. Although the centerpiece of the *Credo* is not a love duet, Bach inserts a movement in this style as well, the third aforementioned movement *Et in unum Dominum* (And [I believe] in the one Lord). Again, the topic of the text is devotion (and that meant, in contemporary theology, love) to Christ and it is expressed in a style that is close to a love duet.

The centerpiece, *Crucifixus*, is followed by *Et resurrexit* (And he rose again), which is composed in the style of a modern concerto and musically "paints" the resurrection of Christ with ascending motives. The adoration of the Holy Spirit (*Et in Spiritum Sanctum*) serves as a point of repose. It is a calm aria, performed by the bass and accompanied by two oboi d'amore. It is a counterpart to the duet *Et in unum Dominum*, since it balances the symmetric outline of the whole Creed:

Choir—Choir—**Duet**—Choir—Choir—Choir—**Solo**—
Choir—Choir

Sanctus

While the first part of the *Sanctus* had been composed in 1724,
the *Osanna*, *Benedictus*, and the *Agnus Dei* were written in the
late 1740s. The *Sanctus* employs a six-part choir, accompanied
by trumpets, timpani, oboes, strings, and basso continuo. Thus,
the movement demands a slightly larger ensemble than the
previous pieces, which only used a maximum of five voices.
Bach's motivation in 1724 to compose a *Sanctus* for six voices
was probably the original biblical context of the liturgical text.
The beginning of the liturgical *Sanctus* is taken from the book
of Isaiah. It is the song of the celestial Seraphim, which have
six wings. The movement is rich with additional number
symbolism. The word "Sanctus" is repeated three times at the
beginning, as it was common in the liturgical text. Bach picks
up on this by using three instrumental groups (trumpets,
oboes, strings), each of which is in itself subdivided into three
individual voices.[38] The main musical subject consists of a long
melismatic line with 8th-note triplets that gradually ascend,
elevating the praise to God in the highest.

The following *Osanna in excelsis* (Praise in the highest)
expands the vocal forces once again. It is a polychoral concerto
for two four-part choirs and instruments. The movement is
based on a chorus from a secular cantata Bach had composed
in 1732 (BWV Anh. I, 11). The *Benedictus* (Be blessed) is an
aria for an unidentified solo instrument (probably the flute)
and tenor. It is one of the most stylistically progressive movements in the mass. The flexible rhythm of both the voice and
the instrument, which is significantly different from the rather

motoric and stereotypical rhythms of the other mass movements, is influenced by the modern sensitive style ("Empfindsamer Stil"). It is as if Bach had wanted to prove his talent in this style.

Agnus Dei

After a repetition of the *Osanna*, the *Agnus Dei* is sung by the alto and accompanied by violins. The movement about the Lamb of God, who died for the sins of the world, is a dialogue between the voice and the instruments that lacks the virtuosic temperament of earlier arias in this mass. The text about the death of Christ was a place for meditation, not for extroverted virtuosity. The movement is a parody of a now lost aria. As mentioned in the previous chapter, Bach took the same aria as a model for his *Ascension Oratorio* BWV 11, from 1735. The text there is "Ach bleibe doch, mein liebstes Leben" (Ah do stay, my dearest life).[39] Both pieces share the lamenting tone and the begging character, which is expressed by chromaticisms in the bass line and leaps that bridge dissonant intervals.

At the end of the composition Bach repeats the *Gratias* from the *Gloria* section, now with the text *Dona nobis pacem* (Give us peace), thus drawing a connection between the older parts of the mass and the newly composed ending. Bach seems to have finished the remainder of the mass without having the same architectural plans in mind that shaped the first parts of the composition. The framework here is not as symmetrical as that of the *Kyrie*, *Gloria*, and *Credo*, and there is no love duet. Bach rather sets the mood and affect of each individual section of the text, without trying to establish an overarching structural plan.

Musical Greatness

The *B Minor Mass* is a showpiece in several respects. At least a third of the twenty-seven movements were borrowed from earlier compositions. But Bach is very careful in the way he re-uses the older pieces. He never parodies two movements from one model, as he does in several cantatas, his *Christmas Oratorio*, or his smaller *Kyrie-Gloria* masses. Furthermore, in several cases, Bach parodies movements in the *B Minor Mass* that had a similar text in the parody original version as in the Latin composition.

Bach carefully integrates the older pieces as well as the new compositions into a new and coherent overarching structural concept. At least in the *Kyrie*, *Gloria*, and *Credo* he creates a symmetrical architecture that is framed by vocal-instrumental movements and that has a Christological section as its center-piece. Most of the movements of the mass might have their own history, but the way Bach combines them is unique and new. The whole is clearly more than the sum of its parts. In the *B Minor Mass* we can see different influences at work. Bach composed the first half of the mass as part of his application for the title as court composer in Dresden. In order to support his application, he used several stylistic devices he knew from masses in the Saxon capital. However, he did not simply imitate them. He combined these devices with his own musical language, the Lutheran orthodox theology in which he had grown up and worked, his own sense for musical architecture, and his propensity for musical drama.

Is Bach's *B Minor Mass* the greatest artwork of all times and all people? Is it the greatest piece by the greatest composer? I am not going to answer these questions. Music is not about better, faster, louder. Instead, I want to return to the one movement that Bach used twice in his mass, the *Gratias agimus tibi*, which returns at the end of the mass with the text *Dona nobis pacem*. The first time we hear the movement, the text praises God's Glory: "We give thanks to you for your great glory." Bach employs trumpets and timpani to create a sonic representation of the splendor of God. The second time around, the glorious music seems out of place. It appears at the end of the *Agnus Dei*, the adoration of Christ as the Lamb of God during the liturgy of the Lord's Supper. "Lamb of God, who bearest the sins of the world, have mercy upon us," finally leads to the plea, *Dona nobis pacem* (Give us peace). The movement, with its percussion, trumpets, choir, and other instruments, is a glorification of God, but of a God who suffered as the "Lamb of God." It is the plea for peace, for wellbeing, for a fulfilled life that can only be hoped for. It is praise in spite of the daily experience of human suffering. It is the hope that the God whose glory had been celebrated earlier, and who as the crucified knows about suffering, will reveal himself in the future as the bringer of peace.

CHAPTER EIGHT

POSTLUDE

Johann Sebastian Bach was about twenty-three years old when he composed one of his earliest masterworks, the funeral cantata *Gottes Zeit ist die allerbeste Zeit* BWV 106, also known as *Actus Tragicus*. The centerpiece of this cantata is an intricate juxtaposition of three distinct layers: the three lower voices—alto, tenor, and bass—sing a motet based on the words from Sirach 14:18, "Es ist der alte Bund, Mensch, du mußt sterben" (It is the old covenant: man, you must die), while the instruments interject lines from the sixteenth-century chorale "Ich hab mein Sach Gott heimgestellt" (I have trusted all my things in God). The third layer in this complex fabric is woven by the soprano. The high voice repeats the words of Revelation 22:20, "Ja, komm, Herr Jesu, komm!" (Yes, come, Lord Jesus, come!) in a mantra-like manner. The cry for Jesus' coming culminates in an emotional outburst towards the end of the movement. The lower voices fall silent, then the instruments drop out, and finally even the supporting basso continuo stops playing while the soprano sings her last plea with an extensive melisma (example 8.1). The cry for Jesus' coming is answered in a later movement by the bass

Example 8.1: Bach, *Gottes Zeit ist die allerbeste Zeit* BWV 106/2ᵈ, mm. 182–5

voice with Christ's words on the cross, "Heute wirst du mit mir im Paradies sein" (Today you shall be with me in Paradise).

   Bach's *Actus Tragicus* is a lesson in the Lutheran art of dying (*ars moriendi*) and it demonstrates how the dying believer can proceed from acknowledging that she has to die to a state of consolation in which she gives herself and her fears over to Christ. The soprano outburst in this example is the turning point in this transition. It is the moment when the singer awaits the coming of Jesus in a heightened emotional state.

Even though the *Actus Tragicus* was composed about a quarter of a century before most of the major vocal works by Bach that I have discussed in this book, the theological framework is still the same. The relationship between divinity and humanity, Jesus and the believer, bridegroom and bride, is characterized by affection and love on both sides. Jesus' sacrificial death is a sign of his love, and the appropriate human responses are love and affection for God and his son. In the *Magnificat*, Bach had composed the *Et misericordia* (And his mercy) in the style of an intimate love duet for alto and tenor. In the *Christmas Oratorio*, the divine mercy that is revealed in the incarnation is again celebrated in an emotional duet for a male and a female voice, this time for soprano and bass. Even in the *B Minor Mass*, Bach uses intimate duets to highlight the Christological texts in the *Kyrie*, the *Gloria*, and the *Credo*.

The ultimate testament to this divine-human love relationship is the death of Christ on the cross at Golgotha. The *St Matthew Passion* highlights this in the aria "Aus Liebe will mein Heiland sterben" (Out of love my Savior is willing to die). The seventeenth-century theologian Heinrich Müller, whose books were known to Bach, had written in his interpretation of the crucifixion, "Your Jesus loves you. Love seeks to be united with the beloved. In order to be united with you, Jesus has united himself with your flesh." And even after the ascension of Christ, the love between Christ and the believer established a continuing bond between the divine and human sphere, as the soprano aria from the *Ascension Oratorio* stresses, "Your love remains behind, so that I in the meantime, here in advance, already restore myself in my spirit by the future glory, when we one day stand before you, there."

In the *Actus Tragicus*, the soprano cries out for the presence of Jesus in the hour of her dying, but the presence of Christ is a recurring theme in all of Bach's major vocal works. Theologians in the seventeenth and eighteenth centuries described the presence of Christ as *inhabitatio Christi*, the dwelling of Christ in the human heart. As I have outlined in the chapter on the *Christmas Oratorio*, Bach's work has two narratives: one is the biblical story of Jesus' birth in Bethlehem, but the second one is the coming of Christ into the believer's heart. We can almost hear the response of the alto in the terzetto from the *Christmas Oratorio* as a response to the plea by the soprano in the *Actus Tragicus*: Come, Lord Jesus—He is already here!

The idea of Christ's presence in the heart manifests itself in different ways in the major vocal works I have discussed in this book: the heart is the manger in which the baby Jesus can rest (BWV 248/9) or the heart is the grave in which the body of Jesus is buried (BWV 244/65). In the image of the heart, two theological images converge: the idea of the divine-human relationship as a love relationship and the continuous presence of the divine in the *inhabitatio Christi*. It is therefore not surprising that images of hearts were ubiquitous in the devotional literature from Bach's time. We have seen one example in the first image from Wiegner's passion meditations from 1724. Others go even further and show Jesus sweeping the sinful heart with a broom; Jesus enlightening the dark human heart with a candle; or Jesus comfortably resting in the human heart.

The texts Bach set in his vocal works often reference the heart as the place of divine presence and Bach's compositions frequently employ a musical language that underscores the affectionate relationship that is expressed by this image: emotional and elegiac arias, seductive lullabies, and almost erotic love duets. Bach had a clear sense for both the dramatic and musical possibilities this theology of love had to offer. Occasionally, he even drew a little heart himself. At the bottom of the score for movement 38 in part four of the *Christmas Oratorio*, Bach ran out of space when he had to write the text for the recitative, "mein Jesus labet Herz und Brust" (my Jesus refreshes heart and breast). Instead of writing out the word for 'heart,' he drew a small heart instead. We should not misunderstand this as a hidden theological message; it was primarily a pragmatic decision. But it demonstrates how Bach was deeply steeped in the devotional imagery of his time and that it came naturally to him to draw the symbol instead of writing the complete word.

This book has tried to weave together three stories. One is the story of Bach's major vocal works. Even though I have not presented them in a strict chronological order, I started with the *Magnificat*, as the earliest example, from 1723, and I ended with the *B Minor Mass*, which Bach completed only a short time before his death in 1750. We have seen some developments in Bach's work, but even more, I have emphasized the elements that connect all these works: their place in the liturgy, the theologies of love and divine presence, and the musical techniques Bach employed to interpret and highlight the texts that were given to him by his librettist.

The second story is the life of Jesus, beginning with Mary's pregnancy, during which she sang the *Magnificat*, and continuing with the *Christmas Oratorio*, which covers the time between Jesus' birth and the arrival of the three wise men. The two passions have provided two theologically distinct views of Jesus' death and the two smaller oratorios for Easter Sunday and Ascension Day have retold the events of Jesus' final days on earth. The narrative of Jesus' life is also the story that provides the chronological framework for the liturgy and the ecclesiastical year: Visitation Day, Christmas, Good Friday, Easter Sunday, Ascension Day. The major events in salvation history are also the anchor points of the Christian liturgy, both in the Lutheran and Catholic traditions. The text of the Latin mass recounts some of these events in the *Gloria* and especially the *Credo*. We have seen how musical elements in Bach's settings of these texts refer back to his compositions in the oratorios and passions.

The third story this book has told, or rather highlighted as a story in Bach's major vocal works, is the love story between Christ and humanity, bridegroom and bride. If there is one theme that returns in every single work discussed here, then it is the human-divine love story: the longing and waiting for the beloved, his arrival, the loving gaze, the kiss, the embrace, the physical consummation of the love, the fear of loss, the complete devastation at the death of the beloved, and the consolation in the moment of his return. It would be easy to construct a gripping love story based on this list and to turn it into a moving opera. The early *Actus Tragicus* from 1708 already gives a glimpse of Bach's talent for telling a moving story. The exuberant outbreak of the soprano at the end of the central movement exhibits some of the emotionality of Bach's later pleas for the bridegroom's arrival in the heart of the bride.

As I have mentioned in the opening chapter, this book can only serve as a brief introduction to works that are so complex that scholars have written thick books on single pieces— without being able to exhaust everything that could be said.

This book is an invitation to listen, to read the texts carefully, and to consider the place the oratorios, passions, and masses had in the course of the church year and the liturgy, but foremost, to enjoy and to marvel at these "small works" of Bach's "science."

APPENDIX

A. Timeline

Before 1720

3/21/1685   Johann Sebastian Bach is born in Eisenach

1708   First performance of *Gottes Zeit ist die allerbeste Zeit (Actus Tragicus)* BWV 106 in Mühlhausen

4/22/1714   First performance of *Weinen, Klagen, Sorgen, Zagen* BWV 12 in Weimar (movement 2 was the model for *Crucifixus* in *B Minor Mass* BWV 232)

1720s

5/22/1723   Bach arrives in Leipzig

7/2/1723   First performance of *Magnificat* BWV 243a (first version in E flat major)

8/1/1723   First performance of cantata *Schauet doch und sehet* BWV 46 (movement 1 was the model for *Qui tollis* in *B Minor Mass* BWV 232)

4/7/1724	Performance of the first version of the *St John Passion* BWV 245
7/2/1724	First performance of the chorale cantata *Meine Seel' erhebt den Herren* BWV 10
2/23/1725	First performance of the secular cantata *Entfliehet, verschwindet, entweichet ihr Sorgen* BWV 249a (model for the Easter cantata *Kommt, fliehet und eilet* BWV 249)
3/30/1725	Performance of the second version of the *St John Passion* BWV 245
4/1/1725	First performance of the Easter cantata *Kommt, fliehet und eilet* BWV 249 (later reworked into the *Easter Oratorio*)
11/27/1725	First performance of the cantata *Auf, süß entzückende Gewalt* BWV Anh. I, 196 (movements served as parody models for *B Minor Mass* BWV 232 and *Ascension Oratorio* BWV 11)
12/25/1725	First performance of the Latin *Sanctus* BWV 232^{III} (later part of the *B Minor Mass*)
4/11/1727	First performance of the earlier version of the *St Matthew Passion* BWV 244
1/1/1729	First performance of the cantata *Gott, wie dein Name, so ist auch dein Ruhm* BWV 171 (movement 1 was the model for *Patrem omnipotentem* in *B Minor Mass* BWV 232)
1729	First performance of the cantata *Gott, man lobt dich in der Stille* BWV 120 (movement 2 was the model for *Et expecto* in *B Minor Mass* BWV 232)

1730s

8/27/1731	First performance of the cantata *Wir danken dir, Gott, wir danken dir* BWV 29 (movement 2 was the model for *Gratias* in *B Minor Mass* BWV 232)
4/11/1732	Performance of the third version of the *St John Passion* BWV 245
6/5/1732	First performance of the cantata *Froher Tag, verlangte Stunden* BWV Anh. I, 18 (movement 1 was the model for the opening movement of the *Ascension Oratorio* BWV 11)
8/3/1732	First performance of the cantata *Es lebe der König, der Vater im Lande* BWV Anh. I, 11 (movement 1 was the model for *Osanna in excelsis* in *B Minor Mass* BWV 232)
1732	First performance of the revised version of the *Magnificat* BWV 243 (D major) (maybe in one of the following years)
7/5/1733	First performance of *Laßt uns sorgen, laßt und wachen* BWV 213 (most of the movements served as parody models for the *Christmas Oratorio* BWV 248)
9/27/1733	Bach sends the first two parts of the *B Minor Mass* BWV 232 (*Kyrie* and *Gloria*) to the Electoral Court in Dresden
12/8/1733	First performance of *Tönet, ihr Pauken! Erschallet, Trompeten* BWV 214 (most of the movements served as parody models for the *Christmas Oratorio* BWV 248)
10/5/1734	First performance of *Preise dein Glücke, gesegnetes Sachsen* BWV 215 (one movement was parodied in the *Christmas Oratorio* BWV 248)

12/25/1734– 1/6/1735	First performance of the six parts of the *Christmas Oratorio* BWV 248	
5/19/1735	First performance of the *Ascension Oratorio* BWV 11	
3/30/1736	Performance of the revised and expanded version of the *St Matthew Passion* BWV 244	
1738	Performance of the *Easter Oratorio* BWV 249 (based on a piece from 1725)	

1740s

1742 and later	Further performances of the *St Matthew* *Passion* BWV 244
4/4/1749	Performance of the fourth version of the *St* *John Passion* BWV 245
August 1748– October 1749	Completion of the remaining parts of the *B Minor Mass* BWV 232
7/28/1750	Johann Sebastian Bach dies in Leipzig

B. Parody Models

1. *Parodies in the Christmas Oratorio BWV 248*

Movement in the Oratorio	Model	Form
1. Jauchzet, frohlocket	BWV 214/1 Tönet, ihr Pauken!	Chorus
4. Bereite dich, Zion	BWV 213/9 Ich will dich nicht hören	Aria
8. Großer Herr, o starker König	BWV 214/7 Kron und Preis gekrönter Damen	Aria

15. Frohe Hirten	BWV 214/5 Fromme Musen!	Aria
19. Schlafe, mein Liebster	BWV 213/3 Schlafe, mein Liebster	Aria
24. Herrscher des Himmels	BWV 214/9 Blühet ihr Linden in Sachsen	Chorus
29. Herr, dein Mitleid	BWV 213/11 Ich bin deine	Aria duetto
36. Fallt mit Danken	BWV 213/1 Laßt uns sorgen	Chorus
39. Flößt, mein Heiland	BWV 213/5 Treues Echo	Aria
41. Ich will nur dir zu Ehren leben	BWV 213/7 Auf meinen Flügeln sollst du schweben	Aria
47. Erleucht auch meine finstre Sinnen	BWV 215/7 Durch die ven Eifer entflammeten Waffen	Aria
51. Ach, wenn wird die Zeit erscheinen	model unknown	Aria terzetto
54. Herr, wenn die stolzen Feinde	BWV 248 VIa/1	Chorus
56. Du Falscher, suche nur	BWV 248 VIa/2	Recitativo [accompagnato]
57. Nur ein Wink von seinen Händen	BWV 248 VIa/3	Aria
61. So geht! Genug	BWV 248 VIa/4	Recitativo [accompagnato]

62. Nun mögt ihr stolzen Feinde schrecken	BWV 248 VIa/5	Aria
63. Was will der Hölle Schrecken	BWV 248 VIa/6	Recitativo à 4
64. Nun seid ihr wohl gerochen	BWV 248 VIa/7	Chorale [=hymn]

Parody models

BWV 213	*Laßt uns sorgen, laßt uns wachen. Dramma per musica. Hercules auf dem Scheidewege* (Cantata for the birthday of Prince Friedrich Christian of Saxony on September 5, 1733)
BWV 214	*Tönet, ihr Pauken! Erschallet, Trompeten. Dramma per musica* (Cantata for the birthday of Queen and Electress Maria Josepha on December 8, 1733)
BWV 215	*Preise dein Glücke, gesegnetes Sachsen. Dramma per musica* (Cantata for the anniversary of August III's election as King of Poland on October 5, 1734)
BWV 248 VIa	unknown cantata, composed around 1734; extant are only violin 1+2 and basso continuo

2. Parodies in the Ascension Oratorio BWV 11

Movement in the Oratorio	Model	Form
1. Lobet Gott in seinen Reichen	BWV Anh. I, 18/1	Chorale
2. Der Herr Jesus hub seine Hände	New composition	Recitative

3. Ach Jesu, ist dein Abschied	New composition	Recitative
4. Ach, bleibe doch	BWV Anh. I, 196/3	Aria
5. Und ward aufgehoben	New composition	Recitative
6. Nun lieget alles unter dir	New composition	Chorale
7a. Und da sie ihm nachsahen	New composition	Recitative
7b. Ach ja! So komme bald zurück	New composition	Recitative
7c. Sie aber beteten ihn an	New composition	Recitative
8. Jesu, deine Gnadenblicke	BWV Anh. I, 196/5	Aria
9. Wenn soll es doch geschehen	New composition	Chorale

Parody models

BWV Anh. I, 18	*Froher Tag, verlangte Stunden* (Cantata for the inauguration of the renovated Thomas School, June 5, 1732 (music lost))
BWV Anh. I, 196	*Auf, süß entzückende Gewalt* (Cantata for wedding Peter Hohmann and Christiana Sibylla Mencke, November 27, 1725 (music lost))

3. Parodies in the B Minor Mass BWV 232

B Minor Mass	Date	Models (if known)
I.1. Kyrie eleison	1733	
I.2. Christe eleison		Very likely parody but model unknown
I.3. Kyrie eleison		

I.4. Gloria		Very likely parody but model unknown
I.5. Et in terra pax		
I.6. Laudamus te		Very likely parody but model unknown
I.7. Gratias agimus tibi		BWV 29/2: *Wir danken dir, Gott, wir danken dir* (1731)
I.8. Domine Deus		
I.9. Qui tollis		BWV 46/1: *Schauet doch und sehet, ob irgend ein Schmerz sei* (1723)
I.10. Qui sedes		Very likely parody but model unknown
I.11. Quoniam tu solus sanctus		
I.12. Cum Sancto Spiritu		
II.1. Credo	1748/9	[earlier version around 1747/8]
II.2. Patrem omnipotentem		BWV 171/1: *Gott, wie dein Name, so ist auch dein Ruhm* (1729)
II.3. Et in unum Dominum		Parody but model unknown
II.4. Et incarnatus		New composition
II.5. Crucifixus		BWV 12/2: *Weinen, Klagen, Sorgen, Zagen* (1714)
II.6. Et resurrexit		
II.7. Et in Spiritum Sanctum		

II.8. Confiteor		
II.9. Et expecto		BWV 120/2: *Gott, man lobt dich in der Stille* (1729)
III. Sanctus	1725	Composed in 1725 as original composition
IV.1. Osanna in excelsis	1748/9	BWV Anh. I, 11/1: *Es lebe der König, der Vater im Lande* (1732)
IV.2. Benedictus		
IV.3. Osanna [=IV.1.]		
IV.4. Agnus Dei		BWV Anh. I, 196/3: *Auf, süß entzückende Gewalt* (1725)
IV.5. Dona nobis pacem [=I.7.]		BWV 29/2: *Wir danken dir, Gott, wir danken dir* (1731)

Known parody models

BWV 12	*Weinen, Klagen, Sorgen, Zagen* (Cantata for Sunday Jubilate, April 22, 1714)
BWV 29	*Wir danken dir, Gott, wir danken dir* (Cantata for the inauguration of the new town council in Leipzig, August 27, 1731)
BWV 46	*Schauet doch und sehet, ob irgend ein Schmerz sei* (Cantata for the 10th Sunday after Trinity, August 1, 1723)
BWV 120	*Gott, man lobt dich in der Stille* (Cantata for the inauguration of the new town council in Leipzig, 1729)
BWV 171	*Gott, wie dein Name, so ist auch dein Ruhm* (New Year's Cantata, January 1, 1729)

BWV Anh. I, 11   *Es lebe der König, der Vater im Lande*
                  (Cantata for the name day of Elector
                  August III, August 3, 1732 (music lost))

BWV Anh. I, 196   *Auf, süß entzückende Gewalt* (Cantata for
                  the wedding of Peter Hohmann and
                  Christiana Sibylla Mencke, November 27,
                  1725 (music lost))

C. Glossary

accompagnato: Accompanied; often used as description of
recitatives in distinction to secco. In an accompagnato
recitative, the singer is accompanied not only by the instrumental bass but also by higher instruments, such as violins,
flutes, or oboes

adagio: Slow

aria: A vocal piece for one (or sometimes more) soloists with
instrumental accompaniment

basso continuo: Foundational bass line with accompanying
harmonies, mostly realized by a keyboard instrument (occasionally also by a lute or another instrument that is able to
play chords)

BWV: Bach Werke Verzeichnis; the catalogue of Bach's works

cantilation: A form of liturgical singing in which a text is
recited based on a given melodic model that can easily be
adapted to different texts

chorale: Protestant hymn

chromatic: A sequence of notes that proceeds in half-tone
steps

concerto: Primarily an instrumental genre in which one
instrument or a group of instruments alternates with a
larger ensemble of instruments. Bach often used this form

in his vocal works as well integrating the voices of the chorus in an instrumental concerto structure

cont., continuo: Abbreviation of "basso continuo"

f., forte: Strong, loud

fugue: A musical genre or part of a composition in which a musical theme ("subject") is treated successively by each of the voices

homophony, homophonic: A musical texture in which the different voices are dependent on each other. Often one of the voices is the main melody while the other voices have an accompanying role

melisma, melismatic: The slurring of one syllable of text over several notes. The opposite is "syllabic"

molt' adagio: Very slow

motet: A vocal genre in which the individual voices move independently (polyphonically); in Bach's time the voices are often doubled by instruments but the instruments do not have independent lines

obbligato: An independent and indispensable line in a musical composition; often a solo instrument in an aria

ostinato: A short melodic pattern that recurs unaltered frequently (often in the bass)

p., piano: Soft, quiet

parody: A reworking of an existing composition, mostly by adapting it to a new text

polychoral: A musical piece or movement that juxtaposes different choirs and/or instrumental ensembles in a dialogue

polyphony, polyphonic: A musical texture in which every voice maintains its rhythmic and melodic independence; the opposite is "homophonic"

pp., pianissimo: Very soft, very quiet

recitative: A vocal genre in which the text is declaimed in a way that approximates natural speech; often only accompanied by basso continuo

ritornello: An instrumental pre-interlude that is often repeated throughout a piece

secco: In a secco recitative, the voice is only accompanied by the basso continuo but not by other instruments

sourdini: Instrument played with a damper, a device to dampen the sound

syllabic: Every syllable of the text is sung to a different note. The opposite is "melismatic"

triplet: Three smaller notes are sung on one beat (instead of normally two); indicated by the number 3 on top of the notes

vivace: Lively

NOTES

Chapter 1: Prelude

1. Anonymous, "Sebastian Bach, and his Musical Compositions," *The New Monthly Magazine and Literary Journal*, Vol I: Original Papers (London: Colburn, 1821), 471. For the wider context of the *Monthly Magazine* see Mark Louis Parker, *Literary Magazines and British Romanticism* (Cambridge: Cambridge University Press, 2000), 135–56.
2. Ibid., "Sebastian Bach, and his Musical Compositions," 471.
3. The view of Handel is not entirely positive. The author concedes that Bach's music has more depth than the works by the British national composer: "In Handel every thing is more plain, lies more to the surface, while Bach is elaborate, profound, and finished in all his productions, from a certain period of his age." Ibid., 471.

Chapter 2: A Female Voice

1. For a detailed overview of Bach's responsibilities in Leipzig see Christoph Wolff, *Johann Sebastian Bach. The Learned Musician* (New York: Norton, 2000), 252.
2. The official beginning of his tenure was May 16, but Bach did not arrive in Leipzig until May 22.
3. An extensive study of the *Magnificat* repertoire in Leipzig was compiled by Robert M. Cammarota, *The Repertoire of Magnificats in Leipzig at the Time of J. S. Bach: A Study of Manuscript Sources*, 2 vols, PhD, New York University, 1986.
4. For the composition date of the first version of the Latin *Magnificat* BWV 243a see Andreas Glöckner, "Bachs Es-Dur-Magnificat BWV 243a – eine genuine Weihnachtsmusik?", *Bach-Jahrbuch*, 89 (2003), 37–45.
5. See Mark Peters, "Meine Seel' erhebt den Herren (BWV 10) as Chorale Cantata and Magnificat Paraphrase," *Bach*, 48 (2012), 34.

6. For the special structure of the liturgy on those days see Chapter Four of this book.
7. Cf. Markus Rathey, "Christmas 1723. Johann Sebastian Bach's Artistic Evolution," *The Choral Journal*, 48 (2007), 14–23.
8. Glöckner, "Bachs Es-Dur-Magnificat BWV 243a," 37–45.
9. The four interpolations in the version from Christmas 1723 were: "Vom Himmel hoch, da komm ich her," "Freut euch und jubilieret," "Gloria in excelsis Deo," and "Virga Jesse floruit."
10. Cf. Beth Kreitzer, *Reforming Mary. Changing Images of the Virgin Mary in Lutheran Sermons of the Sixteenth Century* (Oxford: Oxford University Press, 2004), 54; and Jaroslav Pelikan, *Mary through the Centuries. Her Place in the History of Culture* (New Haven: Yale University Press, 1996), 153–63.
11. Mattias Lundberg's book *Tonus Peregrinus. The History of a Psalm-Tone and its Use in Polyphonic Music* (Farnham: Ashgate, 2011) traces the long and complex history of the psalm-tone and analyzes its use in music history.
12. An excellent interpretation of the gender connotations in Bach's *Magnificat* is given in Wendy Heller's article, "'Aus eigener Erfahrung redet': Bach, Luther, and Mary's Voice in the *Magnificat*, BWV 243," *Understanding Bach*, 10 (2015), 31–69.
13. See Kreitzer, *Reforming Mary*, 50 and 112–14.
14. Heide Wunder, "What Made a Man a Man? Sixteenth- and Seventeenth-Century Findings," in *Gender in Early Modern German History*, ed. Ulinka Rublack (Cambridge: Cambridge University Press, 2002), 21–2.
15. According to reformer Martin Luther, the story of the Visitation sets a model for Christian faith and love as Mary is presented as a humble hand-maiden willing to serve others. See Kreitzer, *Reforming Mary*, 49.
16. Again, Bach employs a musical feature that had already been used by seventeenth-century predecessors.
17. The fact that Bach eventually gives a solo to each of the voices does not contradict our interpretation of gender stereotypes in Bach's arias. In spite of his systematic pattern, he was still free to decide in what order he wanted to use the five voices.
18. For a general overview see Markus Rathey, "Der zweite Leipziger Jahrgang – Choralkantaten," in Reinmar Emans and Sven Hiemke (eds), *Bachs Kantaten. Das Handbuch* (Das Bach-Handbuch 1/1) (Laaber: Laaber-Verlag, 2012), 331–449.
19. The transcription *Meine Seele erhebt den Herren* BWV 648 is part of the *Schübler Chorales*, published in 1748/49. See Peter Williams, *The Organ Music of J. S. Bach*, 2nd edn (Cambridge: Cambridge University Press, 2003), 329–30.
20. For the Lutheran view of Mary in salvation history see Miri Rubin, *Mother of God. A History of the Virgin Mary* (New Haven: Yale University Press, 2009), 367–78.

Chapter 3: From Love Song to Lullaby

1. For Bach and opera see Manuel Bärwald, "Italian Opera Performances in Bach's Leipzig: New Sources and Research Perspectives," *Understanding Bach*, 6 (2011), 9–17; and Michael Maul, "New Evidence on Thomaskantor Kuhnau's Operatic Activities, or: Could Bach Have Been Allowed to Compose an Opera?", *Understanding Bach*, 4 (2009), 9–20.

2. The genesis of the term and concept of "drammi per musica" is outlined by Ellen Rosand, *Opera in Seventeenth-Century Venice. The Creation of a Genre* (Berkeley: University of California Press, 1991), 34–6.

3. English translation quoted after Christoph Wolff, "Under the Spell of Opera? Bach's Oratorio Triology," in Daniel R. Melamed (ed.), *J. S. Bach and the Oratorio Tradition* (Bach Perspectives, 8) (Urbana: University of Illinois Press, 2011), 6.

4. See Markus Rathey, *Johann Sebastian Bach's Christmas Oratorio. Music, Theology, Culture* (New York: Oxford University Press, 2016).

5. "...durch mich soll dein Glanz und Schimmer sich zur Vollkommenheit erheben," BWV 213/7.

6. See Joyce Irwin, "German Pietists and Church Music in the Baroque Age," *Church History*, 54 (1985), 29–40.

7. Martin Luther, "Preface to Georg Rhau's *Symphoniae iucundae*," in *Luther's Works 53: Liturgy and Hymns*, ed. Ulrich S. Leupold (Philadelphia: Fortress Press, 1965), 323.

8. Johann Arndt, *Sechs Bücher vom Wahren Christenthum ... Nebst dessen [Arndt's] Paradieß-Gärtlein* (Altdorff: Zobel, 1735), 641–2 (book 5, chapter 7, § 1).

9. Johann Joachim Neudorf, *Christlicher Unterricht, für die Jugend, wie die H. Advents-Zeit, das H. Christ-Fest und das Neue Jahr GOttgefällig zu feyren sey*. Nebst einer Vorrede von Erdmann Neumeistern (Hamburg: Kißner, [1727]), 5.

10. Johann Christoph *Wenzel, Der unerkandte Jesus zu Christlicher Vorbereitung auf das Heilige Weyhnacht-Fest von der studierenden Jugend in Zittau den 21. December. 1718 in einem kurtzen Dramate vorgestellet* (Budißin: David Richter, 1719), 11; for the complete text recited by *Ratio* see ibid., 47–8.

11. See Markus Rathey, "'Singet dem Herrn ein neues Lied' (BWV 190). Johann Sebastian Bachs Auseinandersetzung mit dem Te Deum laudamus," in Martin Geck (ed.), *Bachs 1. Leipziger Kantatenjahrgang*. Dortmunder Bach Forschungen, 3 (Dortmund: Klangfarben Musikverlag, 2002), 287–301; for a theological interpretation of the cantata within the context of the liturgical and theological understanding of New Year's Day see Jochen Arnold, *Von Gott poetisch-musikalisch reden. Gottes verborgenes und offenbares Handeln in Bachs Kantaten* (Göttingen: Vandenhoeck & Ruprecht, 2009), 405–22.

12. As with all Jewish boys, Jesus was circumcised shortly after his birth. In the tradition of the church this religious act acquired a symbolic meaning as well. The shedding of the few drops of blood during the circumcision was often seen as foreshadowing Jesus' death at the cross.

13. "Und da acht Tage um waren, dass das Kind beschnitten würde, da ward sein Name genennet Jesus, welcher genennet war von dem Engel, ehe denn er im Mutterleibe empfangen ward."

Chapter 4: Divine Glory and Human Suffering

1. James of Milan, *Stimulus amoris*, trans. Michelle Karnes as *Imagination, Meditation, and Cognition in the Middle Ages* (Chicago: University of Chicago Press, 2011), 157.

220   NOTES to pp. 72–104

2. "Mein Herz, in dem die ganze Welt bei Jesu Leiden gleichfalls leidet, die
   Sonne sich in Trauer kleidet, der Vorhang reißt, der Fels zerfällt, die Erde
   bebt, die Gräber spalten, weil sie den Schöpfer sehn erkalten, was willst du
   deines Ortes tun? Zerfließe, mein Herze, in Fluten der Zähren dem
   Höchsten zu Ehren! Erzähle der Welt und dem Himmel die Not: Dein
   Jesus ist tot!"
3. Barbara H. Rosenwein, *Emotional Communities in the Early Middle Ages*
   (Ithaca: Cornell University Press, 2006), 2.
4. The original German text reads, "Mein Hertz entbrenn in Gott, verlaß was
   eitel heißt. Nur dein Gecreützigter erquickt den matten Geist."
5. For the history of these lesser-known works see Daniel R. Melamed,
   Hearing Bach's Passions (New York: Oxford University Press, 2005), 97–130.
6. For the versions and revisions see ibid., 66–77.
7. See Markus Rathey, "Johann Sebastian Bach's *St John Passion* from 1725:
   A Liturgical Interpretation," *Colloquium: Music, Worship, Arts*, 4 (2007),
   123–39.
8. An excellent introduction to the *St John Passion*, including an overview of
   the different versions, is Alfred Dürr's *Johann Sebastian Bach, St John
   Passion: Genesis, Transmission, and Meaning*, trans. Alfred Clayton (Oxford:
   Oxford University Press, 2000).
9. For a thorough study of the 1725 *St John Passion* see Eric Chafe, *J. S. Bach's
   Johannine Theology. The St. John Passion and the Cantatas for Spring 1725*
   (Oxford: Oxford University Press, 2014).
10. See Melamed, *Hearing Bach's Passions*, 135.
11. The original Latin text is: "Ecce, quomodo moritur justus et nemo percipit
    corde. Viri justi tolluntur et nemo considerat. A facie iniquitatis sublatus
    est justus et erit in pace memoria ejus: In pace factus est locus ejus et in
    Sion habitatio ejus. Et erit in pace memoria ejus."
12. For Bach and Brockes see Daniel R. Melamed, "Johann Sebastian Bach
    and Barthold Heinrich Brockes," in Melamed (ed.), *J. S. Bach and the
    Oratorio Tradition* (Bach Perspectives, 8) (Urbana: University of Illinois
    Press, 2011), 13–41.
13. This section is characteristic of the way in which some of the anti-Jewish
    tendencies of the Gospel of John are reinterpreted theologically: while the
    biblical text blames the Jews for the death of Christ, the libretto of the
    St John Passion highlights the believer as likewise guilty. For an extensive
    analysis of Bach's *St John Passion* and the anti-Judaism in the Gospel of
    John, see Michael Marissen, *Lutheranism, Anti-Judaism, and Bach's St John
    Passion* (Oxford: Oxford University Press, 1998).
14. For the dramatic function of chorale tropes like this see Markus Rathey,
    "Drama and Discourse. The Form and Function of Chorale Tropes in
    Bach's Oratorios," Bach Perspectives, 8 (2010), 42–68.
15. See the overview in Melamed, *Hearing Bach's Passions*, 143–7.
16. Heinrich Müller, *Evangelische Schluß-Kett Und Krafft-Kern, Oder
    Gründliche Auslegung der gewöhnlichen Sonn- und Fest-Tags-Evangelien* ...
    (Franckfurt am Mayn: Andreae [etc.], 1734), 1111.
17. See the excellent study by Stephen Greenblatt on the transformation of
    the concept of Purgatory during the sixteenth and seventeenth centuries:
    Stephen Greenblatt, *Hamlet in Purgatory* (Princeton: Princeton University
    Press, 2001).

Chapter 5: The Passion and the Passions

1. *The Athenaeum. Journal of Literature, Science, the Fine Arts, Music, and the Drama*, 2602, September 8, 1877, 314.
2. Ibid., 314.
3. In 1729 Bach used movements from the passion for a cantata for a memorial service for Leopold, Prince of Anhalt-Köthen. The new text for the cantata *Klagt, Kinder, klagt es aller Welt* BWV 244a was written by Bach's Leipzig librettist Picander, who had also written the libretto for the *St Matthew Passion*. The music for the cantata is lost; only the text has survived.
4. The earliest example of such a modern passion oratorio at St Thomas in Leipzig seems to be Stölzel's passion *Ein Lämmlein geht*, performed on Good Friday 1734.
5. Cf. Theodor Mahlmann, "Die Stellung der unio cum Christo in der lutherischen Theologie des 17. Jahrhunderts," in *Unio. Gott und Mensch in der nachreformatorischen Theologie. Schriften der Luther-Agrikola-Gesellschaft*, 35, ed. Matti Repo and Rainer Vinke (Helsinki: Luther-Agrikola-Gesellschaft, 1996), 97.
6. Johann Arndt, *Sechs Bücher vom Wahren Christenthum . . . Nebst dessen [Arndt's] Paradieß-Gärtlein* (Altdorff: Zobel, 1735), 634 (book 5, chapter 3, § 3).
7. Ibid., 641 (book 5, chapter 7, § 1); for the complete German text see Chapter Three of this book.
8. Müller, *Geistliche Erquick-Stunden* (1672); English trans. Isabella van Elferen in *Mystical Love in the German Baroque. Theology, Poetry, Music* (Lanham: Scarecrow Press, 2009), 186.
9. Gerhard, *Erklährung der Historien des Leidens und Sterbens* (1611); English trans. van Elferen in *Mystical Love*, 184.
10. Van Elferen, *Mystical Love*, 191.
11. Quoted after van Elferen, *Mystical Love*, 100.
12. For Luther's understanding of the Lord's Supper as constitutive for the establishment of a Christian community see Markus Rathey, "Eucharistische Ethik in Luthers Abendmahlssermon von 1519," *Luther: Zeitschrift der Luther-Gesellschaft*, 63 (1992), 66–73.
13. Van Elferen, *Mystical Love*, 125.
14. Müller, *Himmlischer Liebes-Küß* (1669); English trans. van Elferen in *Mystical Love*, 208.
15. Arndt, *Sechs Bücher vom Wahren Christenthum*, 634 (book 5, chapter 3, § 3).
16. For a more detailed account of the interconnectedness of love, passion, and the Lord's Supper see the excellent account in Bryan Spinks, *Do This in Remembrance of Me: The Eucharist from the Early Church to the Present Day* (London: SCM Press, 2014), 261–9.

Chapter 6: Seeing and Understanding

1. John Locke, *An Essay Concerning Human Understanding* (1690), eds. G. Fuller, R. Strecker, and J. P. Wright (London: Routledge, 2000), 48.
2. Christian Wolff, *Vernünftige Gedancken von den Kräfften des menschlichen Verstandes und ihrem richtigen Gebrauche* (Halle: Renger, 1713).
3. Ibid., 10.

4. Ibid., 111.
5. For Wolff's metaphysics in the context of his concepts of perception and epistemology see Ludger Honnefelder, *Scientia transcendens. Die formale Bestimmung der Seiendheit und Realität in der Metaphysik des Mittelalters und der Neuzeit (Duns Scotus – Suárez – Wolff – Kant – Pierce)* (Hamburg: Felix Meiner, 1990), 295–381.
6. See Christoph Wolff, "Under the Spell of Opera? Bach's Oratorio Trilogy," in Daniel R. Melamed (ed.), *J. S. Bach and the Oratorio Tradition* (Bach Perspectives, 8) (Urbana: University of Illinois Press, 2011), 1–12.
7. Both the oratorios for Easter and for Ascension Day would also have been repeated during the vespers services in the early afternoon of the feast day.
8. Cf. Eleonore Sent (ed.), *Die Oper am Weißenfelser Hof* (Weißenfelser Kulturtraditionen, 1) (Rudolstadt: Hain Verlag, 1996); see also Renate Brockpähler, *Handbuch zur Geschichte der Barockoper in Deutschland* (Emsdetten: Lechte, 1964), 369–79.
9. Bach also revised the secular cantata another time, in 1726, reworking the music into a birthday cantata for Graf Joachim Friedrich von Flemming (*Verjaget, zerstreuet, zerrüttet, ihr Sterne* BWV 249b).
10. For Bach's Stölzel reception see Peter Wollny, "'Bekennen will ich seinen Namen'—Authenzität, Bestimmung und Kontext der Arie BWV 200. Anmerkungen zu Johann Sebastian Bachs Rezeption von Werken Gottfried Heinrich Stölzels," *Bach-Jahrbuch*, 94 (2008), 123–58; Marc-Roderich Pfau, "Ein unbekanntes Leipziger Kantatenheft aus dem Jahr 1735. Neues zum Thema Bach und Stölzel," *Bach-Jahrbuch*, 94 (2008), 99–122; and Andreas Glöckner, "Ein weiterer Kantatenjahrgang Gottfried Heinrich Stölzels in Bachs Aufführungsrepertoire?," *Bach-Jahrbuch*, 95 (2009), 95–115.
11. The texts differ only in small details; cf. Michael Marissen, *Bach's Oratorios. The Parallel German-English Texts with Annotations* (Oxford: Oxford University Press, 2008), 139, fn. 2.
12. Gottfried Ephraim Scheibel, *Poetische Andachten Uber alle gewöhnliche Sonn- und Fest-Tage, durch das ganze Jahr: Allen Herren Componisten und Liebhabern der Kirchen-Music zum Ergötzen* (Leipzig/Breßlau: Rohrlach, 1725), 76.
13. See Markus Rathey, "Two Unlikely Sisters: The 'Cross' and the 'Crosses' in BWV 12 and 69a," *Bach*, 38 (2007), 1–44.
14. For Bach's library see Robin A. Leaver, *Bach's Theological Library. A Critical Bibliography* (Neuhausen-Stuttgart: Hänsler, 1983).
15. Müller, *Evangelische Schluß-Kett Und Krafft-Kern, Oder Gründliche Auslegung der gewöhnlichen Sonn- und Fest-Tags-Evangelien . . .* (Franckfurt am Mayn: Andreae [etc.], 1734), 1111.
16. Ibid., 1123–4.
17. Philipp Spitta, in his influential nineteenth-century Bach biography, had called the scene with the shroud "tasteless" (Philipp Spitta, *Johann Sebastian Bach. His Work and Influence on the Music of Germany, 1685–1750*, trans. Clara Bell and J. A. Fuller-Maitland [London: Novello, 1889] (reprint New York: Dover, 1979), vol. ii, 591); however, Renate and Lothar Steiger ("... angelicos testes, sudarium et vestes: Bemerkungen zu Johann Sebastian Bachs Osteroratorium," *Musik und Kirche*, 53 (1983)) were able to show that not only the structure of the *Easter Oratorio*, but also this detail, were directly derived from medieval Easter plays.
18. Müller, *Evangelische Schluß-Kett*, 1121.

19. Ibid., 1111.
20. Schulze, *Die Bach-Kantaten. Einführungen zu sämtlichen Kantaten Johann Sebastian Bachs* (Leipzig: Evangelische Verlagsanstalt, 2006), 658.
21. Müller, *Evangelische Schluß-Kett*, 1117.
22. Johann Arndt, *Sechs Bücher vom Wahren Christenthum ... Nebst dessen [Arndt's] Paradieß-Gärtlein* (Altdorff: Zobel, 1735), 641–2 (book 5, chapter 7, § 1). For the German original see Chapter Three of this book.
23. Müller, *Evangelische Schluß-Kett*, 786.
24. Ibid., 1177.

Chapter 7: Between Opera and Architecture

1. Anthony Tommasini, "The Greatest," *New York Times*, January 21, 2011.
2. Announcement in *Leipziger Allgemeine Musikalische Zeitung*, Intelligenzblatt, 3, 1818.
3. George B. Stauffer, *Bach: The Mass in B Minor: The Great Catholic Mass* (New Haven: Yale University Press, 2003), ix.
4. Cf. Walter Blankenburg, *Einführung in Bachs h-moll-Messe* (Kassel: Bärenreiter, 1996), 16–18.
5. Samuel J. Rogal, "For the Love of Bach: The Charles Burney – Samuel Wesley Correspondence," *Bach*, 23 (1992), 31–7; and Michael Kassler and Philip Olleson, *Samuel Wesley (1766–1837): A Source Book* (Aldershot: Ashgate, 2001).
6. Cf. Stauffer, *The Mass in B Minor*, 190.
7. Christoph Wolff, *Johann Sebastian Bach. The Learned Musician* (New York: Norton, 2000), 471.
8. This is true, for example, for an edition of Bach's smaller masses in A major BWV 234 from 1818 and G major BWV 236 from 1828 (both edited by Poelchau); they were not intended as enrichments of the repertoire of liturgical music but as compositional models.
9. Cf. Karen Lehmann, *Die Anfänge einer Bach-Gesamtausgabe: Editionen der Klavierwerke durch Hoffmeister und Kühnel (Bureau de Musique) und C. F. Peters in Leipzig 1801–1865: Ein Beitrag zur Wirkungsgeschichte J. S. Bachs.* Leipziger Beiträge zur Bach-Forschung, 6 (Hildesheim: Olms, 2004); and Markus Rathey, "Bach-Renaissance, Protestantismus und nationale Identität im deutschen Bürgertum des 19. Jahrhunderts," *Protestantische Identität und Erinnerung: Von der Reformation bis zur Bürgerrechtsbewegung in der DDR.* Formen der Erinnerung, 16, ed. Joachim Eibach and Marcus Sandl (Göttingen: Vandenhoeck & Ruprecht, 2003), 177–90.
10. See Celia Applegate, *Bach in Berlin: Nation and Culture in Mendelssohn's Revival of the St Matthew Passion* (Ithaca: Cornell University Press, 2005).
11. The piece was performed by Karl Riedel and the *Riedel-Verein*, Leipzig, cf. Gerhard Herz, "The Performance History of Bach's B minor Mass," *Studies in Musicology*, 73 (1985), 202.
12. *The New Bach Reader. A Life of Johann Sebastian Bach in Letters and Documents*, eds Hans T. David and Arthur Mendel, revised and enlarged Christoph Wolff (New York: Norton, 1998), 151–2.
13. Ibid., 158.
14. Stauffer, *The Mass in B Minor*, 57.
15. Norbert Elias, *The Court Society*, trans. Edmund Jephcott (New York: Pantheon Books, 1983).

16. Ibid., 41–5.
17. Cf. Blankenburg, *Einführung in Bachs h-moll-Messe*, 59.
18. Rolf Dammann, *Der Musikbegriff im deutschen Barock* (Laaber: Laaber-Verlag, 1984), 80–86.
19. Cf. Christoph Wolff, *Der stile antico in der Musik Johann Sebastian Bachs: Studien zu Bachs Spätwerk*. Archiv für Musikwissenschaft, Beihefte, 6 (Wiesbaden: Steiner, 1968).
20. Wolff has pointed out this similarity in his article "Origins of the Kyrie in the B Minor Mass," in Christoph Wolff, *Bach: Essays on his Life and Music* (Cambridge: Harvard University Press, 1991), 141–51.
21. Kirsten Beißwenger, *Johann Sebastian Bachs Notenbibliothek*. Catalogus Musicus, 13 (Kassel: Bärenreiter, 1992), 322–3.
22. For Bach's use of duets in his sacred music see the overview by Mary J. Greer, *The Sacred Duets and Terzets of Johann Sebastian Bach: A Study of Genre and Musical Text Interpretation*, Phil. Diss., Harvard University, 1996.
23. John Butt, *Bach: Mass in B Minor* (Cambridge: Cambridge University Press, 1991), 60–69. A more critical position on Bach's use of concerto form in his vocal music was recently taken by Miriam K. Whaples, "Bach's Recapitulation Forms," *Journal of Musicology*, 14 (1996), 475–513.
24. Cf. Marshall, "Bach the Progressive: Observations on his Later Works," *Musical Quarterly*, 62 (1976), 341.
25. Quoted by Charles Burney, *A General History of Music from the Earliest Ages to the Present*, vol. ii, London 1776–1789, ed. Frank Mercer (New York: Harcourt, Brace and Company, 1935), 736–7.
26. See Alfred Dürr, *The Cantatas of J. S. Bach*, trans. Richard D. P. Jones (Oxford: Oxford University Press, 2005), 731–4.
27. For Bach's parody technique see Hans-Joachim Schulze, "The Parody Process in Bach's Music: An Old Problem Reconsidered," *Bach*, 20 (1989), 7–21.
28. Only the text of this cantata has come down to us, but Klaus Häfner has convincingly argued that the common structure of the texts between the *Domine Deus* and the duet *Ich will/Du sollst rühmen* points to a relationship between these two pieces. Cf. Klaus Häfner, "Über die Herkunft von zwei Sätzen der h-moll-Messe," *Bach-Jahrbuch*, 63 (1977), 56–64.
29. Luther, "Heidelberg Disputation" (1518), in *Martin Luther: Basic Theological Writings*, ed. Timothy F. Lull (Minneapolis: Fortress Press, 1989), 43–4; cf. Jos E. Vercreysse, "Luther's Theology of the Cross at the Time of the Heidelberg Disputation," *Gregorianum*, 57 (1976), 523–48.
30. Cf. Elke Axmacher, *Johann Arndt und Paul Gerhardt: Studien zur Theologie, Frömmigkeit und geistlicher Dichtung des 17. Jahrhunderts*. Mainzer hymnologische Studien, 3 (Tübingen/Basel: Francke, 2001), 217–20.
31. "Der Apostel Paulus vermahnet seinen Thimotheum / daß er stets solle im Gedächtniß tragen Jesum / den Gecreutzigten. [...] Daran erkennen wir seine Liebe / daß er sein Leben hat für uns gelassen / uns zwar / da wir seine Feinde waren. So ists je billich / daß wir Liebe mit Liebe vergelten. Das ist aber der Liebe Art / daß sie das Geliebte stets trage im Gedächtniß. Wie sie gehet und stehet / da erbildet sich das Geliebte in ihren Gedancken. Die wir den Herrn Jesum lieben / sollen ihn auch stets im Gedächtniß tragen. Der gecreutzigte Jesus ist der einzige wahre Trost unserer Seelen." [English translation MR]: Heinrich Müller, *Evangelischer Hertzens-Spiegel / Jn Offentlicher Kirchen-Versammlung / bey Erklärung der Sonntäglichen und*

Fest-Evangelien / Nebst beygefügten Passions-Predigten (Frankfurt: Wust, 1679), 981, quoted after Renate Steiger, *Gnadengegenwart. Johann Sebastian Bach im Kontext lutherischer Orthodoxie und Frömmigkeit*, Doctrina et Pietas II/2 (Stuttgart-Bad Cannstatt: Frommann-Holzboog, 2001) 6.

32. Cf. Stauffer, *The Mass in B Minor*, 82–3.
33. Ibid., 85.
34. Philipp Spitta, *Johann Sebastian Bach. His Work and Influence on the Music of Germany, 1685–1750*, trans. Clara Bell and J. A. Fuller-Maitland [London: Novello, 1889] (reprint New York: Dover, 1979), vol. iii, 50.
35. Luther, "The Small Catechism," in *Basic Theological Writings*, 480.
36. Peter Wollny, "Ein Quellenfund zur Entstehung der h-Moll-Messe," *Bach-Jahrbuch*, 80 (1994), 163–9.
37. Cf. Blankenburg, *Einführung in Bachs h-moll-Messe*, 85–7, and Stauffer, *The Mass in B Minor*, 131–5.
38. The trumpets are accompanied by a fourth instrument, the timpani.
39. Wolff, "The Agnus Dei of the B Minor Mass: Parody and New Composition Reconciled," in Wolff, *Bach: Essays on His Life and Music* (Cambridge: Harvard University Press, 1991), 332–9.

WORKS CITED

Anonymous, "Sebastian Bach, and his Musical Compositions," *The New Monthly Magazine and Literary Journal*, Vol I: Original Papers (London: Colburn, 1821), 467–75

Applegate, Celia, *Bach in Berlin: Nation and Culture in Mendelssohn's Revival of the St Matthew Passion* (Ithaca: Cornell University Press, 2005)

Arndt, Johann, *Sechs Bücher vom Wahren Christenthum . . . Nebst dessen [Arndt's] Paradieß-Gärtlein* (Altdorff: Zobel, 1735)

Arnold, Jochen, *Von Gott poetisch-musikalisch reden. Gottes verborgenes und offenbares Handeln in Bachs Kantaten* (Göttingen: Vandenhoeck & Ruprecht, 2009)

The Athenaeum. Journal of Literature, Science, the Fine Arts, Music, and the Drama, 2602, September 8, 1877

Axmacher, Elke, *Johann Arndt und Paul Gerhardt: Studien zur Theologie, Frömmigkeit und geistlicher Dichtung des 17. Jahrhunderts*. Mainzer hymnologische Studien, 3 (Tübingen/Basel: Francke, 2001)

Bärwald, Manuel, "Italian Opera Performances in Bach's Leipzig: New Sources and Research Perspectives," *Understanding Bach*, 6 (2011), 9–17

Beißwenger, Kirsten, *Johann Sebastian Bachs Notenbibliothek*. Catalogus Musicus, 13 (Kassel: Bärenreiter, 1992)

Blankenburg, Walter, *Einführung in Bachs h-moll-Messe* (Kassel: Bärenreiter, 1996)

Brockpähler, Renate, *Handbuch zur Geschichte der Barockoper in Deutschland* (Emsdetten: Lechte, 1964)

Burney, Charles, *A General History of Music from the Earliest Ages to the Present*, London 1776–1789, ed. Frank Mercer (New York: Harcourt, Brace and Company, 1935)

Butt, John, *Bach: Mass in B Minor* (Cambridge: Cambridge University Press, 1991)

Cammarota, Robert M., *The Repertoire of Magnificats in Leipzig at the Time of J. S. Bach: A Study of Manuscript Sources*, 2 vols, PhD, New York University, 1986

Chafe, Eric, *J. S. Bach's Johannine Theology. The St John Passion and the Cantatas for Spring 1725* (Oxford: Oxford University Press, 2014)

Dammann, Rolf, *Der Musikbegriff im deutschen Barock* (Laaber: Laaber-Verlag, 1984)

Dürr, Alfred, *Johann Sebastian Bach, St John Passion: Genesis, Transmission, and Meaning*, trans. Alfred Clayton (Oxford: Oxford University Press, 2000)

—, *The Cantatas of J. S. Bach*, trans. Richard D. P. Jones (Oxford: Oxford University Press, 2005)

Elferen, Isabella van, *Mystical Love in the German Baroque. Theology, Poetry, Music* (Lanham: Scarecrow Press, 2009)

Elias, Norbert, *The Court Society*, trans. Edmund Jephcott (New York: Pantheon Books, 1983)

Glöckner, Andreas, "Bachs Es-Dur-Magnificat BWV 243a – eine genuine Weihnachtsmusik?", *Bach-Jahrbuch*, 89 (2003), 37–45

—, "Ein weiterer Kantatenjahrgang Gottfried Heinrich Stölzels in Bachs Aufführungsrepertoire?", *Bach-Jahrbuch*, 95 (2009), 95–115

Greenblatt, Stephen, *Hamlet in Purgatory* (Princeton: Princeton University Press, 2001)

Greer, Mary J., *The Sacred Duets and Terzets of Johann Sebastian Bach: A Study of Genre and Musical Text Interpretation*, Phil. Diss., Harvard University, 1996

Häfner, Klaus, "Über die Herkunft von zwei Sätzen der h-moll-Messe," *Bach-Jahrbuch*, 63 (1977), 56–64

Heller, Wendy, "*Aus eigener Erfahrung redet*': Bach, Luther, and Mary's Voice in the *Magnificat*, BWV 243," *Understanding Bach*, 10 (2015), 31–69

Herz, Gerhard, "The Performance History of Bach's B minor Mass," *Studies in Musicology*, 73 (1985), 187–202

Honnefelder, Ludger, *Scientia transcendens. Die formale Bestimmung der Seiendheit und Realität in der Metaphysik des Mittelalters und der Neuzeit (Duns Scotus – Suárez – Wolff – Kant – Pierce)* (Hamburg: Felix Meiner, 1990)

Irwin, Joyce, "German Pietists and Church Music in the Baroque Age," *Church History*, 54 (1985), 29–40

Karnes, Michelle, *Imagination, Meditation, and Cognition in the Middle Ages* (Chicago: University of Chicago Press, 2011)

Kassler, Michael, and Olleson, Philip, *Samuel Wesley (1766–1837): A Source Book* (Aldershot: Ashgate, 2001)

Kreitzer, Beth, *Reforming Mary. Changing Images of the Virgin Mary in Lutheran Sermons of the Sixteenth Century* (Oxford: Oxford University Press, 2004)

Leaver, Robin A., *Bach's Theological Library. A Critical Bibliography* (Neuhausen-Stuttgart: Hänssler, 1983)

Lehmann, Karen, *Die Anfänge einer Bach-Gesamtausgabe: Editionen der Klavierwerke durch Hoffmeister und Kühnel (Bureau de Musique) und C. F. Peters in Leipzig 1801–1865: Ein Beitrag zur Wirkungsgeschichte J. S. Bachs. Leipziger Beiträge zur Bach-Forschung, 6* (Hildesheim: Olms, 2004)

Leipziger Allgemeine Musikalische Zeitung, Intelligenzblatt, 3, 1818

Locke, John, *John Locke: An Essay Concerning Human Understanding in Focus*, eds G. Fuller, R. Strecker, and J. P. Wright (London: Routledge, 2000)

Lundberg, Mattias, *Tonus Peregrinus. The History of a Psalm-Tone and its Use in Polyphonic Music* (Farnham: Ashgate, 2011)

Luther, Martin, "Preface to Georg Rhau's *Symphoniae iucundae*," in *Luther's Works 53: Liturgy and Hymns*, ed. Ulrich S. Leupold (Philadelphia: Fortress Press, 1965), 321–4

—, *Basic Theological Writings*, ed. Timothy F. Lull (Minneapolis: Fortress Press, 1989)

Mahlmann, Theodor, "Die Stellung der unio cum Christo in der lutherischen Theologie des 17. Jahrhunderts," in *Unio. Gott und Mensch in der nachreformatorischen Theologie. Schriften der Luther-Agrikola-Gesellschaft*, 35, ed. Matti Repo and Rainer Vinke (Helsinki: Luther-Agrikola-Gesellschaft, 1996), 72–199

Marissen, Michael, *Lutheranism, Anti-Judaism, and Bach's St John Passion* (Oxford: Oxford University Press, 1998)

—, *Bach's Oratorios. The Parallel German-English Texts with Annotations* (Oxford: Oxford University Press, 2008)

Marshall, Robert L., "Bach the Progressive: Observations on his Later Works," *Musical Quarterly*, 62 (1976), 313–47

Maul, Michael, "New Evidence on Thomaskantor Kuhnau's Operatic Activities, or: Could Bach Have Been Allowed to Compose an Opera?", *Understanding Bach*, 4 (2009), 9–20

Melamed, Daniel R., *Hearing Bach's Passions* (New York: Oxford University Press, 2005)

—, "Johann Sebastian Bach and Barthold Heinrich Brockes," in Daniel R. Melamed (ed.), *J. S. Bach and the Oratorio Tradition* (Bach Perspectives, 8) (Urbana: University of Illinois Press, 2011), 13–41

Müller, Heinrich, *Evangelische Schluß-Kett Und Krafft-Kern, Oder Gründliche Auslegung der gewöhnlichen Sonn- und Fest-Tags-Evangelien . . .* (Franckfurt am Mayn: Andreae [etc.], 1734)

Neudorf, Johann Joachim, *Christlicher Unterricht, für die Jugend, wie die H. Advents-Zeit, das H. Christ-Fest und das Neue Jahr GOttgefällig zu feyren sey*. Nebst einer Vorrede von Erdmann Neumeistern (Hamburg: Kißner, [1727])

The New Bach Reader. A Life of Johann Sebastian Bach in Letters and Documents, eds Hans T. David and Arthur Mendel, revised and enlarged Christoph Wolff (New York: Norton, 1998)

Parker, Mark Louis, *Literary Magazines and British Romanticism* (Cambridge: Cambridge University Press, 2000)

Pelikan, Jaroslav, *Mary through the Centuries. Her Place in the History of Culture* (New Haven: Yale University Press, 1996)

Peters, Mark, "Meine Seel' erhebt den Herren (BWV 10) as Chorale Cantata and Magnificat Paraphrase," *Bach*, 48 (2012), 29–64

Pfau, Marc-Roderich, "Ein unbekanntes Leipziger Kantatenheft aus dem Jahr 1735. Neues zum Thema Bach und Stölzel," *Bach-Jahrbuch*, 94 (2008), 99–122

Rathey, Markus, "Eucharistische Ethik in Luthers Abendmahlssermon von 1519," in *Luther: Zeitschrift der Luther-Gesellschaft*, 63 (1992), 66–73

—, " 'Singet dem Herrn ein neues Lied' (BWV 190). Johann Sebastian Bachs Auseinandersetzung mit dem Te Deum laudamus," in Martin Geck (ed.), *Bachs 1. Leipziger Kantatenjahrgang*. Dortmunder Bach Forschungen, 3 (Dortmund: Klangfarben Musikverlag, 2002), 287–301

—, "Bach-Renaissance, Protestantismus und nationale Identität im deutschen Bürgertum des 19. Jahrhunderts," *Protestantische Identität und Erinnerung: Von der Reformation bis zur Bürgerrechtsbewegung in der DDR*. Formen der Erinnerung, 16, ed. Joachim Eibach and Marcus Sandl (Göttingen: Vandenhoeck & Ruprecht, 2003), 177–90

—, "Christmas 1723. Johann Sebastian Bach's Artistic Evolution," *The Choral Journal*, 48 (2007), 14–23

—, "Johann Sebastian Bach's *St John Passion* from 1725: A Liturgical Interpretation," *Colloquium: Music, Worship, Arts*, 4 (2007), 123–39

—, "Two Unlikely Sisters: The 'Cross' and the 'Crosses' in BWV 12 and 69a," *Bach*, 38 (2007), 1–44

—, "Drama and Discourse. The Form and Function of Chorale Tropes in Bach's Oratorios," Bach Perspectives, 8 (2010), 42–68

—, "Der zweite Leipziger Jahrgang – Choralkantaten," in Reinmar Emans and Sven Hiemke (eds), *Bachs Kantaten. Das Handbuch* (Das Bach-Handbuch 1/1) (Laaber: Laaber-Verlag, 2012), 331–449

—, *Johann Sebastian Bach's Christmas Oratorio. Music, Theology, Culture* (New York: Oxford University Press, 2016)

Rogal, Samuel J., "For the Love of Bach: The Charles Burney – Samuel Wesley Correspondence," *Bach*, 23 (1992), 31–7

Rosand, Ellen, *Opera in Seventeenth-Century Venice. The Creation of a Genre* (Berkeley: University of California Press, 1991)

Rosenwein, Barbara H., *Emotional Communities in the Early Middle Ages* (Ithaca: Cornell University Press, 2006)

Rubin, Miri, *Mother of God. A History of the Virgin Mary* (New Haven: Yale University Press, 2009)

Scheibel, Gottfried Ephraim, *Poetische Andachten Uber alle gewöhnliche Sonn- und Fest-Tage, durch das ganze Jahr: Allen Herren Componisten und Liebhabern der Kirchen-Music zum Ergötzen* (Leipzig/Breßlau: Rohrlach, 1725)

Schulze, Hans-Joachim, "The Parody Process in Bach's Music: An Old Problem Reconsidered," *Bach*, 20 (1989), 7–21

—, *Die Bach-Kantaten. Einführungen zu sämtlichen Kantaten Johann Sebastian Bachs* (Leipzig: Evangelische Verlagsanstalt, 2006)

Sent, Eleonore (ed.), *Die Oper am Weißenfelser Hof* (Weißenfelser Kulturtraditionen, 1) (Rudolstadt: Hain Verlag, 1996)

Spinks, Bryan D., *Do This in Remembrance of Me: The Eucharist from the Early Church to the Present Day* (London: SCM Press, 2014)

Spitta, Philipp, *Johann Sebastian Bach. His Work and Influence on the Music of Germany, 1685–1750*, trans. Clara Bell and J. A. Fuller-Maitland [London: Novello, 1889] (reprint New York: Dover, 1979)

Stauffer, George B., *Bach: The Mass in B Minor: The Great Catholic Mass* (New Haven: Yale University Press, 2003)

Steiger, Renate and Lothar, "... angelicos testes, sudarium et vestes: Bemerkungen zu Johann Sebastian Bachs Osteroratorium," *Musik und Kirche*, 53 (1983), 193–202

Steiger, Renate, *Gnadengegenwart. Johann Sebastian Bach im Kontext lutherischer Orthodoxie und Frömmigkeit*, Doctrina et Pietas II/2 (Stuttgart-Bad Cannstatt: Frommann-Holzboog, 2001)

Tommasini, Anthony, "The Greatest," *New York Times*, January 21, 2011

Vercreysse, Jos E., "Luther's Theology of the Cross at the Time of the Heidelberg Disputation," *Gregorianum*, 57 (1976), 523–48

Wenzel, Johann Christoph, *Der unerkandte Jesus zu Christlicher Vorbereitung auf das Heilige Weyhnacht-Fest von der studierenden Jugend in Zittau den 21. December. 1718 in einem kurtzen Dramate vorgestellet* (Budißin: David Richter, 1719)

Whaples, Miriam K., "Bach's Recapitulation Forms," *Journal of Musicology*, 14 (1996), 475–513

Wiegner, Abraham, *Nöthige Freytags-Arbeit, Oder Catechetische Fragen, und Zwey und funfzig geistreiche Andachten über die Heil. Paßion Jesu Christ. Nach welchen Eine iede durch das Blut Jesu theuer erkauffte und den gecreutzigten Jesum hertzlich-liebende Seele aus schuldiger Danckbarkeit Jeglichen Freytag im gantzen Jahre Zum seeligen Gedächtniß-Tag ihres leidenden und sterbenden Heylandes machen, Oder an jedem Freytage allemahl ein gewisses Stücke des Leidens Jesu in Frage und Antwort deutlich erlernen, mit einer besondern Andacht sich darüber belustigen, und in einem schönen Kupffer das grosse Schmertzens-Bild zugleich sich vor die Augen legen kan* (Leipzig: Martini, 1724)

Williams, Peter, *The Organ Music of J. S. Bach*, 2nd edn (Cambridge: Cambridge University Press, 2003)

Wolff, Christian, *Vernünftige Gedancken von den Kräfften des menschlichen Verstandes und ihrem richtigen Gebrauche* (Halle: Renger, 1713)

Wolff, Christoph, *Der stile antico in der Musik Johann Sebastian Bachs: Studien zu Bachs Spätwerk*. Archiv für Musikwissenschaft, Beihefte, 6 (Wiesbaden: Steiner, 1968)

—, "Origins of the Kyrie in the B Minor Mass," in Wolff, *Bach: Essays on His Life and Music* (Cambridge: Harvard University Press, 1991), 141–51

—, "The Agnus Dei of the B Minor Mass: Parody and New Composition Reconciled," in Wolff, *Bach: Essays on his Life and Music* (Cambridge: Harvard University Press, 1991), 332–9

—, *Johann Sebastian Bach. The Learned Musician* (New York: Norton, 2000)

—, "Under the Spell of Opera? Bach's Oratorio Trilogy," in Daniel R. Melamed (ed.), *J. S. Bach and the Oratorio Tradition* (Bach Perspectives, 8) (Urbana: University of Illinois Press, 2011), 1–12

Wollny, Peter, "Ein Quellenfund zur Entstehung der h-Moll-Messe," *Bach-Jahrbuch*, 80 (1994), 163–9

—, "'Bekennen will ich seinen Namen'—Authenzität, Bestimmung und Kontext der Arie BWV 200. Anmerkungen zu Johann Sebastian Bachs Rezeption von Werken Gottfried Heinrich Stölzels," *Bach-Jahrbuch*, 94 (2008), 123–58

Wunder, Heide, "What Made a Man a Man? Sixteenth- and Seventeenth-Century Findings," in *Gender in Early Modern German History*, ed. Ulinka Rublack (Cambridge: Cambridge University Press, 2002), 21–49

INDEX